Robert Robinson

The Dog Chairman

Allen Lane

ALLEN LANE
Penguin Books Ltd
536 King's Road
London SW10 0UH

First published 1982

Copyright © Robert Robinson, 1982

The Acknowledgements on page 11
constitute an extension of this copyright page

ISBN 0 7139 1477 7

Filmset in Monophoto Baskerville by
Northumberland Press Ltd, Gateshead, Tyne and Wear
Printed in Great Britain by
Richard Clay (The Chaucer Press) Ltd,
Bungay, Suffolk

For
Nick, Lucy
and Suzy

Contents

Contents

Contents

Acknowledgements

Some of these pieces appeared originally in the *Observer*, *High Life*, *The Times*, the *Listener*, *Punch* and the *Sunday Times*. I am grateful to the editors for permission to reprint them. The words of Vladimir Nabokov are copyright in his name, and I am indebted to Mme Véra Nabokov and to Weidenfeld and Nicolson for permission to publish the interview – his last – in which they were spoken. My interview with Alexander Solzhenitsyn is included in this collection by his kind permission. I am most grateful to Jorge Luis Borges for my interview with him that appears in these pages.

The Dog Chairman

Being on the telly, you're in a funny position – not famous, just current. So the telephone rang and I put down the spoon I was just going to eat a boiled egg with and picked up the phone, and a man said, 'Good morning to *you*. My company is making a series of commercials, and we think you'd be just the man to put them over.'

When I see a journalist or a commentator – someone who gets his living forming opinions about things – when I see such a man staring at me out of an advertisement and urging me to buy something because he says so, I always think poor bastard. Because as I meet his level candid gaze, I know he is only in the advertisement because he has agreed not to be impartial. Whereas in the newspaper or on the television he gets his living by guaranteeing exactly the opposite.

He has killed the goose that lays the golden eggs, so that there is no particular reason to go on believing a word he says. As a commentator all he hired out was his capacity to form opinions, but as an advertiser he is hiring out the opinions themselves – henceforward, how are you going to tell when he's doing the one rather than the other?

So apart from hating advertisements the way other people can't stand cats, I reckon I'm showing sound business acumen in never doing them.

'Just the man,' said the fellow at the other end of the telephone. He spoke as if he had an Iron Jelloid stuffed up each nostril.

It was chilly (I was standing in my underpants), I knew the egg was going to get cold, and all I had to do was say no. But there is a certain sort of pleasant manner you can't bear to leave intact.

'How do you mean, just the man?'

He worked a chuckle in under the Iron Jelloids – it must have been one of the most all-purpose chuckles in the world.

'Believability, my dear sir,' the man said.

I started walking up and down as far as the telephone cord would let me.

'But look here,' I said. 'Isn't believability just the quality I'd turn out not to have if I did your commercial? Isn't just the man just *not* the man, the minute he turns up in an advertisement?'

'Say again?'

I caught sight of the egg uneaten on the other side of the kitchen and like a damn fool I went on talking. I wanted him to know I was irritated.

'What sort of commercial, anyway?'

'We-e-e-ell,' said the chap, managing to imply that he knew he was dealing with a pretty shifty customer, yet not letting it affect his big robust friendliness, 'I am not at this time empowered to let you know the name of the actual dog food.'

I know it sounds as if I'm making it up, but this conversation really took place.

'We're keeping it under wraps,' said the man. 'Until the launch.'

A spasm of rage shook me.

'Supposing I don't like dog food,' I shouted.

'Ha-ha-ha. I knew you were right for it. You see, your role would be the Chairman.'

'Look, Mr – '

'I'm Nigel Itching-Higgins.'

'You ring me up at breakfast time to ask me to be a Dog Chairman – ' I broke off. The sun was shining through the kitchen window and lighting up my kneecaps as I stood there in my shirt-tails. Someone in the heart of advertising land had said Robinson is our man. He is a Dog Chairman.

'Listen,' I said. 'I'll stay quiet this end, and you just go on talking.'

For the first time since the exchange had begun, Nigel sounded less confident. He snuffed the Jelloids up a bit further.

'Well, of course we haven't got the technical details absolutely ironed out yet, but roughly the thing is we've got this ventriloquial gimmick and – um – we get the dogs to talk.'

'Well, they can say it.'

'Say what?'

'Say – don't you know what you want them to say?'

'They need a Chairman, you see,' said Nigel, suddenly a little desperate, as if he too were beginning to realize what all this would sound like to a human being. 'To encourage them. Draw them out. Hullo, Fido, what do you think of the – ah – biscuits?'

'What does Fido think of them?'

'Oh. Well. He says he likes them. Naturally.'

'I was just wondering how he was going to put it.'

Silence.

'Go on,' I said.

'Well,' said Nigel miserably, 'they thought they might get him to say – ' He petered out.

'Go on,' I said, because the egg was stone cold by this time.

'Woof, woof,' said Nigel, the Iron Jelloids imparting a nice touch of the Pekingese. 'Yum, yum, grr, grr, yeeeowwww ...'

'Does this imply approval?'

'He'll wag his tail,' said Nigel, a bit breathless but brightening up, perhaps at the thought of the first rational bit of dog or other psychology he had so far been able to produce.

'Are you wagging your tail?'

'Say again?'

The Dog Chairman. A famous twentieth-century phantom. Amiable in public, with dogs, for money. Pray silence for your Dog Chairman. Or a more saturnine ghost, a myth for quelling dachshunds. Towser – do you want me to send for The Dog Chairman? A whine of fear. Mother, it's The Dog Chairman. Hush, child, there is no such thing.

'Why did you ask me?'

Nigel became brisk but confidential. He knew that we were both men of the world.

'You see, when we get actors to do this sort of thing, people do tend to think they are only doing it for the money.'

I said, 'And if I had agreed to do it, what do you think I would have been doing it for?'

Nigel went 'ha-ha-ha' in a sort of stylized way, as if he were being careful to relish a species of black humour which, for all he knew, might be current in my set. I put the phone down and stood spellbound in my kitchen. I felt a small glittering fragment from the giant lie had fallen like a meteorite into my own backyard, and, throwing the cold egg into the waste-bucket, I raced upstairs to the typewriter, anxious to preserve the evidence before it should crumble in the daylight.

Jorrocks in Ewell

I hired a horse in Ewell. I had a vaguish feeling that a distant suburb might take the unpredictability out of the enterprise, though it didn't seem right to be looking a horse up in the Yellow Pages. I thought a horse based in Ewell might not have the red insane eyes that I think of as natural in horses, and I felt the balmy airs of Ewell might have had a calming, even a debilitating effect on the beast they hired out to me, and what I'd get would have all the reliability of a Volvo, but with four legs.

As we left the stables, the ancient party in charge of the yard said to me, 'If he tries to roll over, just give him a flick with your crop on the tip of his right ear.' I laughed heartily, not wanting to seem unfamiliar with what was obviously an old joke among horse-lovers. As we moved slowly down Fruitwood Crescent, I was torn between thinking I cut a pretty figure and hoping this didn't encourage the young woman in charge of the group to think she was boring me by going too slowly – while the horses are walking you can't tell the difference between me and Nimrod: it's when they start going a bit faster that the fraudulence of my boots and breeches becomes apparent.

I was gravely acknowledging the respectful greetings of the peasantry as they leant out of their primitive bungalows crying, 'Get off and milk it,' when all of a sudden we clopped off the nice safe asphalt and found ourselves in a ploughed field and the ugly beast I'd been trundling along on started throwing its head about as though now we were coming to the bit *he* liked.

One by one the others took off down the path that ran through the middle of the field, and then it was my turn, or more accurately the horse's turn, and he shot away like a high-speed goods train and then after a bit he slowed down as though he were approaching a station. He veered off the path and into the field and the others shouted something, but the horse was now doing an old-fashioned waltz, going sideways and backwards across the furrows, and suddenly I realized what the man at the yard had said was no joke but an actual piece of advice, but it was too late.

We were going down like the *Titanic*, and solemnly, gracefully, the horse and I landed on our backs, he with his legs in the air, me with mine. I'd like to know how you aim at the tip of *anyone's* right ear when you're falling from what seems an eight-storey building; but as I went home with the mud of Ewell plastered all over me, I had a curiously contented feeling, as though for all my efforts to exclude the unpredictable, I was glad I hadn't succeeded.

Aiming, Shooting and Missing

'I dare say you know the sort,' said the other customer in the gun shop. 'Blazes away at low-flying pheasants. Dammit, if you're going to call that sport, you might as well stay at home and take pot-shots at the Rhode Island Reds on the home farm.'

A salesman, who looked a bit like Arthur Treacher, placed himself at a sporting distance from me, clasped his hands behind his back and rocked gently up and down on his heels. What I'd heard made me feel I was in deeper water than I'd been banking on, because up till then it wasn't low-flying pheasants I'd aimed at so much as ones that had actually landed – birds going for strolls on the A30 – and my weapon had been the motorcar. Several times I'd had my wheels up a grassy bank, trying to down one of the succulent creatures with a left and right from the near-side hub-caps. I felt my face getting red, and the other customer looked at me narrowly.

'I – er – hear that guns from Czechoslovakia aren't bad – ' There was a crash as the other customer dropped his matched Purdeys. He shied as he hurried out of the door, scenting a parvenu.

Arthur Treacher smiled. 'Well – ' He fetched a gun out of the rack, hefting it in one hand like a butcher wondering whether to give you the scraps for nothing or charge you fourpence. 'Hear that?' he said as he opened and closed the action with a flourish. 'Just like a dustbin-

lid going back. Look at the carving on the grip. Probably done with
a knife and fork by an old lady living in the Carpathian Hills. They
do it like my granny does her knitting, watching the telly at the same
time. I wouldn't use that gun,' Arthur Treacher said, bringing to a
close this lightning tour of his similes and his prejudices, 'for anything
but spreading ready-mixed cement.'

I dashed off to Scotland Yard to expedite the licence, scooped up
the gun from Arthur who condescended to receive payment for it, and
bore it off to the country feeling dreadfully potent.

'Is that what you take when you go out *killing*, Dad?' my small
daughter asked, profoundly approving. With some unction I explained that I wasn't going to kill anything I didn't mean to eat, a
red herring which suitably obscured the more basic question whether
my standard of marksmanship would not for ever protect me from
such a moral dilemma: obscured it, I should say, from all save my son,
a boy with a touch of the sphinx about him, who offered to consume
uncooked anything I hit, up to and including water buffalo.

Actually, I wasn't terribly interested in bringing anything down,
only in the possibility. I don't like going for walks in the country
because it is so easy to turn round and go home again that you can't
help wondering whether it's worthwhile setting out in the first place.
There are no *limits* in the business of going for walks – rather like golf:
you hit the ball, and if it doesn't go far enough you just hit it again,
and if that doesn't work you hit it again, and so on, with nothing to
make you feel that fewer strokes, rather than many, really matter
(whereas with tennis, hit the ball wrong, and the mistake comes back
at you over the net). I thought a gun might lend consequence to a
walk, it might be an object round which a walk could accumulate,
and you'd find yourself doing uncomfortable things like climbing
through hedges and getting brambles in your eyes without it ever
occurring to you – as it always does when you're just out for a stroll
– that you don't have to.

I had this vague idea that it was pigeons I was going to slaughter
– the only pheasant in our neck of the woods being an ancient bird
who each night marched bad-temperedly into the hen-house at Lower
Farm, pushed a hen off its perch and roosted asthmatically in its place
till dawn. But in the light of me having to eat everything I shot, I
wasn't too happy about it being pigeon – when did you last choose
pigeon at a restaurant? Answer, never, on the grounds that you know

it's going to chew like elastic bands. And I had a premonition that if I did manage to down one, it would turn out to be not a wood pigeon, but one of those unshaven meths-drinking Trafalgar Square birds drying out in the country for the weekend.

But I was committed to shooting at something edible, and I set off with my special country hat (wrested from the head of a man I met driving a yoke of oxen down Bond Street), slid unhandily over the wall at the end of the garden and started across the meadow to the copse below. The buttercups had barely stained the tops of my wellies when I heard a sound I knew – a derisive rasp, a tinny trumpeting – and there in the lane at the side of the field I saw the hideous moustachioed face of the man they call The Pill blowing rudely into one of those tin cigars which make a noise like a comb and paper.

I'd been wrong-footed by the chap from the moment I'd had the bad luck to run across him relieving himself against my wall as though he were doing the flints a favour. Indeed, he had so much the air of conferring ducal status that I found myself sneaking through my own garden gate as though my credentials wouldn't bear inspection. Just A Minute, Just A Minute, he roared, buttoning up and approaching me like a gamekeeper who'd copped a poacher. He let me off with a caution that time, and withdrew playing Colonel Bogey on his lousy gazooka. But a couple of nights after, his face floated up in the twilight outside the kitchen door, and swaying slightly he invited me to drive him home. When I said how far and he said a mile and I started to get the car keys, my wife looked at me as if I'd taken leave of my senses. I can only say that although I had this dim sensation of being the sort of punter con men like him dream about, his very presence seemed to cast me into a light trance.

He announced (as though he'd been doing care work) that he'd passed the day at Taunton Races, and trying to rid myself of the 'fluence I said I hope you won. I Have Never Put A Shilling On A Horse In My Life, he said severely. He made Taunton Races sound like Taunton Assizes at which he had presided as Lord Chief Justice, and all I could come back lamely with was, 'Why do you go, then?' He answered, as though my question had led us into a world far beyond tomfools like me, To See Some Men. Going down the garden path, he was full of the conditions under which he would accept what he had importuned, *viz*. How Fast Do You Drive, I Am Not Sure Your Wife Is Happy About This – even making a feint of going back into the house for her reassurance. He offered me a fag, and when – in another weightless attempt to get my identity back into phase in the face of the man's appalling command of any ridiculous situation he might prescribe – I said, 'No, I don't want to get cancer,' he said, I Will Introduce You To A Doctor.

So when I heard the gazooka, I made a rude gesture and crashed into the copse to kill the pigeons. No luck, of course, and I didn't really mind. I bore them no animus, indeed if the eating business hadn't been paramount, I'd sooner have been banging away at the sort of birds who make facetious noises when a man is working in his garden. To someone sweating with exasperation as pieces of rock keep rolling out of the dry stone wall he is trying to repair, it quickly becomes apparent that the wise thrush doesn't sing each song twice over lest you should think he never could recapture the first fine careless rapture, he sings it twice because he is a dumb thrush and didn't get it right the first time.

Paranoia in the ascendant, I went deeper into the wood. And suddenly I froze. In our part of the country, there are deer. There was a rustle in the boscage ahead of me – a crackling noise – a distant brown shape. My heart beat faster – if I could bring down a stag! I raised the gun, then lowered it. I wanted to be sure – supposing it was a cow? Looking slightly to one side, I saw there was an open ride: if I snook out on to the path, then chucked a stone, the deer would break cover too – and I'd have him. I moved as in a dream, found a piece of rock, and heaved it.

There was a fearful noise, like the word 'Aaaaaargh!' when you see it coming out of the mouth of someone in a cartoon, and up from the undergrowth galloped The Pill. Whether he had been snuffling for truffles I know not, but as he dashed out crying 'Don't shoot!' I was about to lower the gun when I realized (rather like Mr Winkle who saw the reflection of his own cowardice in the eye of Mr Dowler) how things stood, and I put up the weapon again. With a howl, The Pill disappeared into the canebrake, and as I walked home I thought to myself I shouldn't care to eat him, casseroled or otherwise, but if that's the last we see of him, the gun's paid for itself already.

Hockney and His Dad

Hockney was telling me his dad does imitations of the Emperor of Japan and actually takes his teeth out to get the proper effect. At the end of the performance, which is a fairly disobliging one, Hockney's dad puts his teeth back in and says (of the Emperor), 'Ah well, I suppose he can't help it.' Hockney says his father keeps several pairs of false teeth, one set in a jar marked BEST PAIR, another marked NEXT BEST and a third marked NOT BAD. He also keeps things other people might not and has a collection of dud batteries. He gave Hockney a fibre-tipped pen refill which he had labelled PARTLY USED.

Now, I'm very fond of this sort of information, what I like about it is its irreducibility. You can stare at it till the cows come home and it won't get you a degree in sociology. You can't use it for secondary purposes, you can't generalize it away, it isn't *like* anything. I find this cheering because it really is quite easy to walk out into the street and see nothing that isn't a reference to something else which isn't a reference to something else – you wouldn't call it a code because you can crack a code, it's much more an endless jargon, a sort of equation that simply refers to another equation.

So on those odd occasions when you do seem to have arrived at a destination, it's very reassuring. While Hockney was telling me about his dad, I was feeling like our Mr Satchell who used to do the electrics when we were first married. Once he'd got the flex sticking out of the little holes in the plaster where he was going to put the wall-lights, Mr Satchell made sure the electricity was getting through by grabbing hold of the bare wires. 'Ha-a-a-ah,' he would cry – it was a noise midway between a shout of delight and a groan of satisfaction – 'the supply – it's there – it's there – ' I had exactly the same feeling when hearing about Hockney's dad's false teeth. Hockney stood looking at the canvas he was working on and for a moment seemed to speak with his father's voice when he said, 'I sometimes wonder if this is a way for a man of forty to pass his time.'

He'd been talking about Bradford (he's a Bradford man) and art school, and I said that reminds me of the first picture I ever bought. I got it from Bonham's when they were hammering off canvases that had accumulated over the years in the basement of the Royal Academy, a great pile of pictures people had said they'd buy but never got round to paying for, or stuff the painters hadn't bothered to collect when the exhibitions closed – sort of *salon de refusés*, in a way. The one I bought was a big tall picture with two little girls and a mum. They're standing in a road under a bleached-out winter-evening sky, and the perspective is staked out with black telegraph poles all the way down to the dark warehouses at the end of the street. Now, the street is a Bradford street because it says so on the back, and I've always had a feeling – something about the carefulness of the way the painter brought the thing together, the hint you get of an anecdote or story in the way the three figures are standing – that this is exactly the sort of picture people at art schools paint, full of feeling but a touch literary. God knows who the artist is, he's got his name on the back too: D. S. Stafford. Hockney looked incredulous. 'You're joking aren't you? D. S. Stafford was my teacher . . .'

Now, if you were making that story up, you'd have to tear the edges a bit, make them ragged, it's too neat, too pat to be anything but the truth. Hockney's coming to see the picture and he's bringing D. S. Stafford with him. It's rather odd that I've been intimate with D. S. Stafford for twenty years yet never thought of him as a person. Will he mind about the way I came by the picture? Will it enrage him that I only gave eight quid for it? ('You ought to be ashamed of yourself,' J.B.P., another Bradfordian, growled when he heard the price.) Well, I do believe such clear, round, flawless coincidences don't roll out of your turn-ups half often enough – I keep putting off making an actual date with the two painters because after that it will all be over.

Football as Exorcism

On football days in suburbs, the very brick is cramped and wrathful. Railings shake furiously in their stucco, and the tarmac steams with annoyance.

'Ar–sen–oool . . .'

'Li–ver–puuule . . .'

Small parks where the leaves fall early alternate with sweet-shops run by women who hate their customers. On casement ledges in bay-windows, tomatoes left to ripen get greener.

'Ar–sen–oool . . .'

'Li–ver–puuule . . .'

The gravel in side-roads crunches even when the road is empty, and churches made of dark stone look like filled teeth that would love to get back into the toothache business.

'Ar–sen–oool . . .'

'Li–ver–puuule . . .'

The great wailing noise is vengeful, as though all the people in the world had got together to shout back at a hostile universe. The heels of men hurrying to get there in time ring like an army with an edge on its appetite, and policemen on horses circle warily in cul-de-sacs.

'The Brazilian jungle,' said a commissionaire watching the stone terraces fill, 'is perilous, and I leave at half-time. Up the Reds, they'll have cut heads.'

Nobody, according to a series of white notices that might have been put up by the United Nations, would be allowed in if they were carrying sticks. Anyone found with a bottle would be put out of the ground – 'whether the bottle be empty or full' added the rubric, sourly assured that a thirst was no guarantee against other, stronger appetites. Fragments of quartz glistened spitefully in the concrete of the terraces, and men who looked like dog-handlers stood silently facing the crowd.

'We are the grea–test . . .'

Mindless and melancholy, the chanting was a sort of a hymn and, like all hymns, sounded utterly defeated. The crowd sang of glory and victory in exactly the same way a congregation sings of happiness and death: as though they didn't believe it, as though they sensed they were victims, doomed to placate the tyrannous unknown.

'Ar–sen–oool . . .'

'Li–ver–puuule . . .'

A mournful cry, followed by the raising of scarves in unison. The dog-handlers shifted from foot to foot, and policemen prowled the margins of the field. Twenty-three minutes before the game began, the first man was ejected. Five coppers took him away, protesting feebly but looking happy in a daft sort of way, as though he'd done his bit. The animus crackling in the air of the suburb like an electric storm had condensed above his head, and he had been a willing sacrifice.

The linesmen came out, dapper men, the referee followed, more dapper yet, and then all the noise the crowd could muster crashed like Niagara on the two teams as they pranced on their toes aptly into the arena. But the funny thing was this: at that moment, and from that moment on, the menace that the crowd brought with it diminished. Something that had seemed to threaten on the cosmic scale – some universal resentment, brought to the boil by this warlike rendezvous in the stone wilderness – had, with the advent of a tangible conflict, been reduced to the measurable. What might have atomized the identities of all vanished with a roar into the ritual of the game, and what you heard thereafter was a chronic, continuous complaining, a purely domestic dissatisfaction with players who were never going to be able to do for the shouters what the shouters weren't able to do for themselves.

'*Adjust your truss.*'

'Oh, dear me. Oh, dear me.'

'Kick it, Roger – you're in the team.'

'*Wipe your lipstick off, you're a big girl now.*'

'Oh, dear me. Oh, bloody blimey.'

'Harry Kirry, Harry Kirry, he's passing the ball backwards. Oh, you silly player.'

'It comes of wearing plimsolls, ain't they.'

'*You 'omosexual dragonfly.*'

The referee was a saturnine unforgiving man, who ran with his back bent and his eyes close to the ground and threw up his arms at every infringement as though exorcizing, without much hope, the inequity of the world. But even he seemed close to the melting mood when one of the Liverpool players headed the ball into his own goal, as neat as you please. The concerted groan that came from every throat had a muted quality – as though for once the onlookers had been taken aback, as though for once they realized they were watching not the image of their own frustration, but someone real. Even his enemies in the red shirts tousled his hair in deepest sympathy as he opened his mouth and screamed into the void.

And the breath of the whole crowd was taken away when a Liverpool player with an open goal before him was arrested – actually grabbed by the arms, and restrained – by a member of the other team. The roar was the roar of innocence outraged. One spectator laughed at the impudence of the offender, and the man behind him said with a terrible, serious passion, 'You should know better than to laugh at a thing like that.'

Some people started to leave five minutes before the end. They left early, able to dispense with the last little bit because they knew no miracle was going to happen. The walls of routine still stood, in spite of all the shouting, but men at bus-stops looked placid, and the peanut-sellers cried their wares as if they were no longer selling bombs.

Epiphany

Slap at the traffic lights, a chap in a Daf Variomatic drew into the kerb, stopped the car and got out. The man behind him in a Jag hooted and the Daf man walked towards him with a sort of inquiring expression that had a hint of the inverted commas about it. 'Move up, how can I pass you?' shouted the Jag man. 'Rowlocks,' said the Daf man quietly, no respecter of persons, 'I'm parking here. You move back.' Jag man nearly had a seizure. Alongside the Jag was a large lorry, waiting for the lights. The driver, feeling like it, leant out of his cab and said in a languid way to the Jag man, 'You silly old sausage' (or words to that effect) 'why don't you do what he tells you? All the same you Jag drivers, think you own the bleedin' roads.' Jag driver stares at the lorry driver in amazement – lorry bears the name of firm of which he, the Jag driver, is Managing Director! Bereft of speech. Lorry driver continues in same leisurely vein, 'You miserable old turtle, driving them big cars goes to your 'ead, ain't they?' Managing Director gets out of Jag and walks slowly up to lorry driver, steam rising from the top of his head. 'Would you be speaking to me like that if you knew who I was?' I heard him cry. Driver of lorry says, 'I don't care a footle who you are, big 'ead.' 'In that case,' says the Managing Director, 'let me tell you: I am Managing Director of,' and he told him. 'Oh, Castor and Pollux,' exclaims driver, 'goodness me, sir, I really must apologize, don't know what came over me,' etc. 'We won't go into that now,' says the Managing Director, still suffering from what looks like terminal frustration, but plainly amazed at his stunning good luck in having the universe deliver over to him a victim when he was most in need of one. Gets back into his own car, emotionally dislocated, and backs straight into a taxi waiting patiently behind. *Exeunt omnes.* I nearly got out and gave him the five pounds I'd willingly have paid for the seat I'd enjoyed for nothing. The whole thing was a sort of vision.

On Being Embalmed

I wrote a piece about waiters for the *Observer* and ten years later it showed up again, killed, skinned and stuffed, as Question 3 in a paper from the Cambridge University Local Examinations Syndicate, designed to test candidates for their Certificate of Proficiency in English. There was a distinct smell of the path. lab. in the way they'd laid it out, the numbering of the lines especially giving the prose a look of something that had had to have its jaws wired together.

Section B

3. Read the following passage, and then answer the questions which follow.

We treat waiters in a special way, circumspectly, like teenagers or the old – groups with whom our relations are uneasy, anxious, unresolved. In the

On Being Embalmed

company of waiters we are never quite ourselves: relinquishing ordinary speech, we engage in dialogue, as though one actor were rehearsing with another at the first reading of a play, when neither party knows who will turn out to be the villain.

'You recommend the broccoli, waiter?' – brisk, severe, but somehow supplicatory. 'Excellent today, sir' – dubbing you a connoisseur. 'A few potatoes, sir?' murmuring as though he had known you all your life, was your respectful intimate, had been honoured with your confidence, knew your liking for that rare vegetable the potato, had shipped them for you from Samarkand. And as he walks away, just for a second you wonder: What does he think of me?

Doubtful of him, we become doubtful of ourselves. When he brings the food, we start to attitudinize. We pretend he is invisible and don't say thank you. Or we say thank you all the time, as though he were to be placated. After meals we tip to preserve ourselves from the unknown consequences of not tipping. Or we tip meanly, thinking we shall soon be out of range. Or we tip too well, lingering a little to receive from him the assurance that we crave. And sometimes, when we say goodbye to a waiter, we say it in just that intimate, confidential tone he used when he took our order – as though indeed we had been master and man for many a year, and our goodbye was a sort of gift, and we were conscious of our beneficence. But it is always too late: by the time we are ready to accept his opening premise he has already begun to withdraw, he has already begun to abandon us.

Sometimes the unease that permeates the relationship is resolved in a burst of emotion, as though uncertainty were no longer to be borne. Once I asked a waiter for some butter and he yelled, 'Get it yourself!' I nearly burst into tears, but the waiter danced away as blithe as a man who has at last jumped over the edge of the tantalizing cliff and resolved his relationships once and for all.

Tension builds up because client and waiter both feel that their roles won't quite hold water. In form, their relationship suggests that time has stopped round about 1910. But if too much weight is placed on this form, the substance will be found to have changed. Both parties know this, and their joint feelings of schizophrenia charge the relationship with anxiety and dissatisfaction. A predicament of this nature can only be solved by time: but if you grasp its mechanics you can learn to live with it.

Robert Robinson in the *Observer*

[a] Why is the writer's choice of the word 'dialogue' in line 4 so effective?
[b] What aspects of the character of waiters as seen by the writer emerge from the second paragraph?
[c] Why does the writer speak of potatoes as a 'rare vegetable' (line 11)?

[d] Explain how the sentence 'Doubtful of him, we become doubtful of ourselves' (line 14) acts as a link between the ideas expressed in the second and third paragraphs.

[e] How does the author explain the motives behind a customer's various ways of tipping?

[f] In what way do the words 'yelled', 'burst into tears', 'dance' and 'blithe' (lines 28–9) contribute to the point the writer is trying to make in this article?

[g] How far does the last paragraph restate the ideas used in the first?

[h] What solution to the problem he has described does the writer look forward to?

Who expects this sort of scrutiny? I'd have felt like a man in hospital surrounded by students, except in this case there wasn't supposed to be anything wrong with me, there was supposed to be something wrong with them. But can a writer trust a certificate of health handed to him by an examination board? If you write something that will stay still long enough for others' mobility in the language to be measured against it, doesn't that mean that like all specimens it's dead? Those eight questions they ask are a sort of coffin, and I think they might have asked me before assuming I would climb in.

A Door Opening

Towards the end of the couple of years I spent being a film critic during the 1960s I was beginning to feel a special sort of fury. The 80 per cent of what I saw that was rubbish didn't seem to *mind* being rubbish, yet I had to treat it as though it were trying to be something else. The films seemed to think they had no obligations, but there was I, still having to pay attention. You'd have whole movies supplied direct from Fortnum and Mason, complete with Audrey Hepburn, and you wouldn't know where the chandeliers ended and the scenario began. Natalie Wood had a corner in urchins, walking into the end-credits with streaks of clean dirt on her nose, and wearing the radiant look of one who was going to ask for shorter hours and better pay. Mad scientists were putting souls back into bodies with the aid of jam-making equipment, and the Rappaho (played by the Rappaports) swept out of the back-projection as the elements were tattering Phyllis's clothing but decently sparing her bra. Clint Eastwood had just perfected the trick of falling asleep with his cigar still alight under the blankets, prior to waking up and shooting four men dead simultaneously (I remember a feature-player jumping up from behind a hedge and saying with manifest lack of conviction, 'You shot all four of them. I saw you do it.' We saw him do it, and we didn't believe it either). Richard Harris and Richard Widmark and two hundred commandos were concealing themselves behind a telegraph pole or other obvious refuge, invisibility conferred upon them by that magic pair of wire-cutters, while Sidney Poitier – by just standing there and being handsome – was getting a classful of teenage footpads to give up the garotte and go on day-trips to the V and A.

It was like collecting Green Shield stamps: you'd come out into Leicester Square feeling you'd need two million of the things before they'd add up to anything you could cash. And then one morning I walked into the Paris Pullman in Drayton Gardens. I was savagely wondering what sort of bloody old horsehair sofa I was going to have to go ten rounds with that Tuesday (my resentment had a specially roped-off corner that was reserved for foreign films). Anyway, the lights went down and the film started, whereupon the screen turned into a door and the door opened and I walked through it and I found myself in the land of the living.

The film was called *Intimate Lighting*. In the two years I was paid to watch films it was the only film I went to see twice, the only film I felt a mysterious obligation to pay *them* to get into. From the first frame the director seemed to put you into the thing; it was as though you were watching a life you had once led and somehow forgotten.

Simple set-up: a weekend in the country outside Prague, two guests from the big city – a professional cello-player and his young girlfriend – and they're staying at the house of the cello-player's old chum. This chum (now a schoolmaster) is pretty handy with the violin because once upon a time he too was a student of music at the same *conservatoire* as his friend: he shared the same ambitions, but perhaps he wasn't good enough (ah, but how that goes against the grain of the film – everyone is good enough) and so relapsed into domesticity (*relapsed* – wrong again, for in the film there is a sequence in which music by Mozart is scored against domesticity, and domesticity plays the finer tune).

A Door Opening

There's a kind of party to begin with, since the village is turning out for the funeral of some ancient neighbour, the weekend guests of course invited, cortège winding through the cornfields, and a brass band and a few accordions letting go with the sort of ageless lament that is really a solemn raspberry blown in the face of a universe which laid all this upon us. Slapping the tin dashboard of the Czech equivalent of a Morris Minor, the granddad – father-in-law of the host – cries, 'People play different games, but sorrow is the same everywhere.' He stares impassively at the svelte backside of the girlfriend who has elected to walk in front of the car with the mourners. 'You know the saying, "You could travel the world with one sad song"? Ah,' after a pause, 'if this car ran on tears.' He has already approved the cellist's choice of girlfriend, explaining when they stop by the roadside for a pee that he himself had had his leg over in this very field of rye. 'Only it's not rye,' says the son-in-law, and all three men look at each other blank-faced, as though the remark mattered, and then again, didn't.

After the obsequies, the party. A small fat man, ravished by drink, balances a glass of spirits in each hand and belts out an impromptu on the order of *Trees*, while the girlfriend drags the cellist outside to get him in the teeth of his own embarrassment to tap out the words I LOVE YOU on the car-hooter. Old dames in black kerchiefs are beginning to leave and file past the car, looking in through its windows with a special diffidence, as though in encountering someone else's privacy, they had recognized something of their own.

Late lunch. Chicken a bit scraggy. One of the children squawls because he didn't get a drumstick. 'Look at granddad, he didn't get one either, and he's not crying.' Granddad glowers at the nasty bit on his own plate. Girlfriend gives hers to child, hostess gives hers to girlfriend, grandma passes hers to hostess, and granddad switches with girlfriend on the grounds that his nasty bit will be easier for her to cut. The child knocks over a glass of beer, and suddenly, as though the flow of ordinariness had burst open and revealed some exquisite disproportion, the girl starts to laugh and can't stop. She runs out into the kitchen where a mild old gent who has just come to the back door with a fiddle under his arm says, 'I am the local pharmacist. Retired, of course,' and the tears of mirth run down her face. The old fellow's turned up for a spot of music, and while the girl's laughter rings round the house, he goes into the dining-room where the three men are still gloomily trying to down the chicken, and tries out a few bars on his instrument, sitting on the sofa watching them, interested but not wanting to interrupt. The exquisite disproportion is of course identity itself.

And this is where the Mozart comes in. The meal doesn't end, it's transfigured, the community of the table turned into the community of the music as we fade through to the four men having a go at a Mozart quartet. But this time identity is proclaimed because identity is subdued – to the patterns of the music. Not perfectly subdued, since son, father-in-law, guest and visitor grunt and carp as they play ('That was a D.' 'Never.' 'You played a D.' 'Not I.'), but the uneven edge this tears on the proceedings makes it even clearer what's going on: each man, lost in his own mystery, is yet open to the mystery of the others. And then the director goes one better. He re-formulates what we're listening to in visual terms, as the three women – girlfriend, mother, grandma – tiptoe in perfect time along the landing to peep into the bedroom where the children lie asleep. Where does the music really come from? Is it prescribed by Mozart, or is it – in all its grave optimism – prescribed by the people in the house?

The pharmacist – playing the viola – speaks over the music as he plays: 'I love this passage, gentlemen.' Turning to the cellist: 'Dear colleague – may I call you that?' – these days the cello-player is a famous soloist. The cello-player, who has the long empty face of an early bicyclist, nods without taking his attention out of the music, and when I saw this I knew I'd been offered the key in which the film is conducted. No one in the whole world has ever not been a soloist, though famous doesn't come into it.

Well, there's a lot more I haven't told you about. But the last scene is this: Sunday lunch on the little terrace. Grandma produces one of her egg-nogs for pudding. The cellist and the host have awful hangovers. The stuff's in the glasses, so everyone stands up as though it's a toast, and raises the glasses. But the mixture's too thick and it won't come out. 'Patience,' says grandma, 'it's worth waiting for.' They stand with the glasses upended over their mouths, waiting. Silence. 'Oh these Sundays,' groans granddad, and the camera pulls out and the film freezes, and that's the end.

Ivan Passer, once the colleague of Milos Forman, was the director of this film, and it was his debut. I wondered rather about the title – *Intimate Lighting* – thinking it a bit awkward. But on reflection I think he could hardly have called it anything else, lit as it is by the light we sometimes glimpse falling from windows high up in other people's lives. And specially so, since this time the window is pushed up and someone calls us in, and when we enter, the room is our own.

Try a Grasshopper

Leisure is work you volunteer for. I know this because I decided to take up fishing again, and the minute I framed the thought I experienced a sense of fatigue similar to what I imagine the man felt when he said to his wife, 'Wake me early tomorrow, I'm going to start building the Forth Bridge.' I'd still got the rods, but I couldn't find the gear, so I set off for the angler's heartland which is Earlsfield and said briskly, 'I want a reel, a line and a few flies.' 'Ah,' said the bloke behind the counter, 'how heavy's the rod? Six, six and a half?' I groaned and said to him, 'I somehow knew I wasn't going to be able to come into your shop and say what I want and walk out with it. I'll come back tomorrow after I've been to the library.'

But in the fifteen years I haven't been fishing, the books on the subject have come to rest on as many ambiguities as you'd find in a piece on economics in the *Guardian*, and after leafing through one or two I knew enough not to know what to ask for. One particularly maddening commentator on the sport multiplied the entities by saying, 'If you're not having much luck, try a grasshopper.' It wasn't enough you had to find the fish, you had to find a grasshopper as well. That left you wondering whether it was all right to use your hat to catch the grasshopper or whether a true sportsman always lured the insect with a Tupp's Indispensable and a number eight line.

Modelling Session

The male model was of the saturnine order. He was tall and dark, and wore a macintosh and a trilby hat. While the photographer was reloading, he moved his eyebrows fiercely up and down – but in an absent-minded way – and the trilby hat rocked backwards and forwards on his head.

'Now I want you to *enjoy yourselves* – ' the photographer's voice rose threateningly ' – I want you to *have a good time*.' He paused for an instant, then emitted a strangled scream – 'Aaaaaargh' – and took the picture.

'Dreadful,' he said sincerely. 'Maurice, you had a very nasty look on your face. You had your nasty look on.'

The tall model was at the centre of the group, staring into the eyes of a pretty girl in green. Beside him were two small men, two medium-sized men, and a man whose face looked like the bright red seal on a sheepskin indenture. Each held a glass of beer aloft, raised in an attitude of frozen approbation.

A furry man in shirt-sleeves explained the scene to an onlooker: 'People want to feel real. We want to remind them of their earth roots. That's what beer's all about.' He sounded faintly desperate, like an astrologer of old who believed in, but could not quite explain, the sources of his knowledge.

'Reg,' said the photographer, baring his teeth in impatience, 'you're pouring it into Harry's ear.'

The photographer looked tousled about the head, as if he'd just got out of bed, but it was from ducking under the bit of black cloth. 'Interested, Reg, look interested – '

The furry man nodded towards the two very small men and, lowering his voice slightly, said, 'We get them from museums.' The footsteps of small boys echoing in wide floorpolish-smelling rooms, scuffling past glass cases of small men, expertly labelled. But he only meant they worked there. 'They can dodge out for half an hour in their off periods, and they come cheaper and better than the professionals.'

'I said interested, Reg,' cried the photographer furiously from inside the black cloth, 'not bloody amazed –'

The tall model stared into, and right through, the eyes of the pretty girl, going absent for a moment while the camera was fettled. The furry man said to the photographer, 'On the whole, I think the two bald ones ought to have hats. I don't want people thinking that beer makes your hair drop out.'

'Open your eyes, Reg,' urged the photographer, in menacing tones, 'open them, Reg. No, no, not one at a time, *both at once.*' He turned to the pretty girl. 'Undo your knees, darling, and give me one of those private little smiles.' He ducked under the cloth. 'You two at the end, where did you get all those teeth from? This isn't a toothpaste ad, cover 'em up.'

A girl with a short skirt flitted in and out of the studio on tippytoes, bearing messages, coffee, rolls: a member of the household, a free spirit. She glanced at the models, trapped in the prison of having to look human rather than be it, and celebrated her freedom by being nice to a commissionaire.

'It's a special world,' said the tall model soberly, as the furry man called for more beer and went round topping up the glasses. 'Endless journeys to the cleaners with my leisure wear, corduroys, yachting clothes. One specializes, you know. I found I did fit rather comfortably into a bowler hat – the out-of-focus chap in the background, looking yearningly at the girl. And I do hands. I doubt if most people would understand. My uncle lives in Camberley. I tell him, "I have my photograph taken".'

A museum man slept on a chair, seized by the warmth of the studio as by the languors of the mammal room, legs crossed, hands in pockets, chin drooping.

'I'm just a shape,' the tall model said, 'stared at in the Tube, nameless. I turn the pages of magazines and come across myself smiling. Who am I? When the photographer groups the models, I edge towards the back, into the shadow. I'm not mad about being seen. What is it, to be seen and not known?'

'Take off that white wristwatch, darling, will you,' the photographer said to the pretty girl. 'I don't think they would wear a thing like that in Stoke-on-Trent.'

'Where's the loo?' said the pretty girl.

'Face-fatigue is the hazard,' the tall model said, 'a used-up face will kill everyone in the end.'

'Back to work,' shouted the photographer. The museum man awoke, the tall model drifted out of the shadow into the arc-light. His manner was hooded, remote.

'Happy, happy, happy,' cried the photographer, taking a succession of trial prints with his Polaroid. He showed them to the models, and they clustered round the pictures as eagerly as though they were holiday snaps just back from the chemist.

'Now we'll do it,' said the photographer. 'I don't want you smiling this time, Reg, because you're the one who's telling the joke. Move closer to Maurice, darling. If he touches you, just scream. Now – *laugh.*'

They laughed with hearty dolour, bright sadness. They laughed frantically as though perhaps the beer were a poisoned chalice which, by the command of a sadistic emperor, they must drink and seem to enjoy. Their smiles flew at the camera like sling-shot, flaming arrows, cups of boiling lead.

'Aaaaaaargh,' screamed the photographer. 'Maurice, you're doing your *nasty* smile.'

The Diva

Incidental pleasures at Covent Garden – not on the stage, but in the Grand Tier. It was *The Marriage of Figaro* and every time the soprano swam up to a top note or thereabouts, a great fat dame in raspberry bombasine who was sitting behind me went off like a phrase-book with the cork half out. '*Oh, ça alors!*' she sneered venomously. '*Incroyable!*' '*Ah, non – ma foi – ça, c'est trop!*' Evidently a super-annuated diva who'd sung the role herself and wasn't too keen on anyone else having a crack. In the first interval they fetched the big man in the mulberry livery to tell her she had to shut up or get out. Well, she was rather noisy, but I had such a pain down the side of my neck from turning sharp left to look at the stage that I suppose I was in the mood for a little dissent. The seats had cost fifteen quid a head, meaning you got a perfect view of the man's head who was getting a perfect view of the man's head who was getting a perfect view of the man's head in front. I wouldn't have minded this so much if the rest of the audience hadn't given the impression of being people for whom no night at the opera was complete *unless* they went home with a pain in the neck. I mean, there was a good deal of free-floating worship going on: they not only looked to a man as though they didn't mind missing their dinner (which they were certainly going to do, since the performance had a touch of the slow bicycle race about it), they looked as though they would miss it joyfully. So it's possible that the carambas of the *diva* were more acceptable to me than to the rest.

After the second interval she quietened down (I offered a burst of silent applause for her marvellously stoical nephew, a lad of about eighteen who sat beside her and never by so much as a look or a blush let on about how awful he thought his aunty was), though she still simmered, and I found myself increasingly taken up with what didn't matter, like whether or not the Count was wearing a jockstrap and counting the mouldings in the outer architrave of the proscenium arch (not easy – I should be glad to have confirmation that there are, looking stage right, twenty precisely, to the red velvet on the ledge of the third tier). I wasn't exactly turning against Mozart, but what I had suspected for a long time was becoming a certainty – that Mozart is too refined for opera, that there isn't any Mozart opera that wouldn't sound better re-scored as a sequence of symphonies or *concerti*, and that while he does his best to get down on all fours with those who came after him, he never convinces you that he's anywhere near as common as Verdi, Rossini, Donizetti, who were to turn opera into the vulgar treat it really is.

When the curtain came down the *diva* gave a loud and derisive sigh – 'Pfuiiiiii' – and waltzed out. If ever I saw a non-religious member of an opera audience, she was it. Her awful lack of loyalty was, I have to admit, like a warm poultice to my aching neck.

Sightseer's Ankle

There's a peculiar sort of ache that comes on in my ankles when I've been in a department store for anything longer than about ten minutes. I start to feel like a man who's done a day's manual labour, and long to collapse into one of those bentwood chairs they used to provide for old ladies. Well, that's all very well in Selfridges, but what makes me feel slightly guilty is the way I get exactly the same symptom in cathedrals.

I'm as keen and eager as the next sightseer (my wife) when we set out for Florence or Siena, quivering with anticipation when the mint humbug of the Duomo shows up on the horizon, and when I actually arrive I slide vibrantly inside like someone who's fearful the *quattrocento* may try and make a break for it before he's had a chance to pin it to the mat. But in ten minutes I'm experiencing this sense of throbbing fatigue, and all the Romanesque mosaics, all the Bellini statuary, all the illuminated missals, seem to be making a single loud monotonous drumming noise and I have to switch off, looking up at the dome and thinking if you could just haul the chandelier back into the high gallery over the main door and get your legs round it, what a hell of a swing it would make from one end of the nave to the other. I am roused from this reverie by the same words every time – 'Now, let's just put our heads into the Baptistry' – and petulantly demand to go away and look for English newspapers.

So what I'm saying is that sightseeing isn't really as uncomplicated as it might seem; and if you look closely at people who are doing it, you will spot what Henry James spotted when he was watching a bunch of Americans shuffling around the National Gallery – 'their faces,' said Henry, 'bearing expressions of resentment, humanized by fatigue.' As a sightseer, what gets to you after a time (my own threshold is ten minutes but this varies with the individual, ten seconds – or even *minus* ten seconds in acute cases – extending to days or even years with onlookers who are naturally passive), what destroys the morale, is the way the actual sight – the cathedral or the ruin or the stately home or the collection of Duccios – goes on making its enormous statements without effort, leaving all the work to be done by you. The fact that it did an awful lot of work a long time ago just in order to be the Mona Lisa or the Pyramids doesn't soften the lopsidedness of the present arrangements, whereby you are in a ferment of response and it just sits there. This is what makes you feel you've been trying to run straight up the sides of a house.

There is no easy solution, but what we have to get to grips with is the question of guilt. The anxious look that flits across the faces of sightseers in, say, Leningrad is not, as you might suppose, provoked by fears that the surly inhabitants are going to report them to the police if they so much as smile, but a mysterious conviction that it is sinful not to see everything – every picture in the Hermitage, every turret in the Peter and Paul Fortress, every last gilded finial in the palace at Pushkin, not to mention the schools, the University, the battleship and the Kirov Ballet. This is the universal neurosis of the hard-core sightseer – he feels it is shameful if he leaves anything out (symptoms that are often accompanied by camera-mania, in which the victim suffers pangs of conscience if he returns home with a single frame unexposed).

One way of breaking yourself of the compulsion is to note how the people who actually live among the sights never look at them – the Leningrader hurrying past the Winter Palace may register the fact out of the corner of his eye, but his preoccupation is with getting to the dry-goods store to check the rumour that a consignment of toilet rolls has arrived. I sometimes think that may be the only way of looking at anything: the caves at Lascaux, the Golden Gate, the palace of Teotihuacan, all seen out of the corner of your eye, part of a life rather than a reason for it.

Still, that's a counsel of perfection, and I don't expect people who eat twelve Pietàs before lunch to believe me when I tell them it will ruin their teeth. But pending the revolution, one or two of the more irritating conventions might be got rid of. Couldn't we do without French guides – the ones in the château country particularly? Those endless monologues they give are a sort of winding-sheet that you have to lift up and peep under if you want to see Chambord or Azay-le-Rideau. Actually, I'm rather against guides in general. There's a wonderfully restored eighteenth-century house in Royal Crescent, Bath, but when they first opened it it was staffed by a horde of good women, and as you entered each room, your interest rising with the elegance of your surroundings, they grounded it at a blow, insisting you listen to what they thought of it. Any attempt to edge out of earshot met with a sharp reprimand – I hope they are now running tea-shops. All I want when I trail around the average stately home is a simple typewritten sheet stuck on one of those wooden bats – it doesn't get between you and your own imagination.

Perhaps the best sort of sightseeing is when you don't know that's what it is. One afternoon my wife and I strayed into a little Tuscan town – more of a biggish village, really – perched on top of one of those hills that always look so romantic in the background of fifteenth-century pictures. We lounged about the winding streets, admired the fairy-tale towers, and liked it so much we decided to come back in the evening. They were doing *Rigoletto*, an open-air performance in the town square. We took our seats on the wooden benches, underneath the walls of tall houses strung with coloured lamps, where old dames were leaning out of windows. During the interval the cast drank with the audience in a neighbouring café, and when the show started up again an old gentleman sitting beside me wept when Gilda was stabbed, as though seeing it all for the first time. That's what we felt too, as though everything – town included – had come about spontaneously, and we'd had the luck to be present.

Boasted about 'discovering' the place, only to find (of course) that we'd wandered into the ever popular chart-topping Tuscan show-stopper, San Gimignano. It was a bit like claiming to have discovered J. Lyons or the Taj Mahal. But I was delighted. I'd had all the pleasures of a tourist shrine without knowing that's what it was. I'd thought the place was real – and there hadn't been the slightest twinge in either ankle.

Buying a Picture from Lowry

On 6 August 1962, about four o'clock in the afternoon, I bought a picture from L. S. Lowry. I was sitting in the back room of his house in Mottram-in-Longdendale and he was showing me what he'd been painting, setting them up on his easel and saying, 'Hey, hey, I keep on doing them, don't I?' There was one he'd shown me early on, a small single figure, a girl in a black dress and red shoes. I plucked up courage and asked him how much the little pictures fetched, and he said, 'Oh, they go very well, forty pounds or thereabouts.' I asked him if he'd let me have another look at the girl with the red shoes, and I told him it reminded me of my wife in old photographs, long before I knew her.

He swung it up again and studied it. 'Yes,' he said, 'I think I like her, I think I do. Poor little thing, poor little thing.' I was rather shy. I asked him when it might come on sale. 'Oh, it probably won't, it probably won't – why, do you like it? What do you want to give me for it?' I said (going a bit hot in the face) that it was up to him. 'Well, they fetch forty.' We looked at it again and he went on talking. 'Give me thirty for it if you like.' I said I didn't want to get it at cut rates. 'Wait a bit, then, forty with the frame, you'll have to get it framed yourself, forty minus the frame. Give me thirty-five then. Is that a fair price?'

Then he said, 'Shall I sign it for you?' He dodged about looking for a brush, dipped it into a rather dry bit of black on his palette. 'This is the hardest part,' he said. He painted the letters, then incised them with a penknife. 'I'll put the date on the other side, balance it up a bit, you know. I'll put 1960, it's easier to paint. I think I started it in 1956. Shall I wrap it up? I've got a bit of brown paper here.' He went out and got the paper, and as he was doing the wrapping he picked up a sketch he'd done in biro on a lined pad, a drawing of two people, and said, 'I'll *throw it in*. It's only a note, you know, I find I do these things in the street. I'll throw it in. I'm very pleased you like her. Can you see where I've painted over the –?' He broke off and it occurred to me he thought I might not like a painting that you could see had been altered. But he went on, 'I painted her dress red first but I didn't like it, so I painted it over black and left the red shoes, and the red underneath gives the black a very nice quality. There was a lot of work went into that. Oh yes, all out of my head, you know.'

I had to send him a cheque because I didn't have enough money with me at the time, and when he wrote back thanking me for what he called 'the enc.' he said, 'I'm glad the poor little thing has found a good home.' I wrote all this down the day afterwards, and stuck it on the back of the picture so that my children will know all about it. I wrote an article about Lowry, and it elicited the following letter from someone who read it:

I am a portrait painter, one of that tribe who hates parting with paintings, so I hoard them. My brother was the same – maybe a case of not much savvy.

Well, the thing is, I once felt I needed a Lowry painting. My brother was a friend of his. I gathered together my money, all of twenty-five pounds and a few shillings, and set off from Euston. I got there, a shabby enough young woman, and knocked at the door and Lowry opened it and looked at me. We looked at one another for a minute then I said, 'I've come to buy a painting. I paint too but I won't sell any. But I'm telling you this so you won't feel too badly at having to say I can't have one.' And I added I had brought my money.

He said to come on in and we had some tea. Then he brought a picture out and said, 'You can have this one,' so I emptied my purse and gave him the lot. It included my extra for a cup of tea and bus fares but who cared or thought – well, we didn't. He didn't count it, so didn't know what I'd poured out on the table. Then I left. We were alike really.

I walked to the station and got into the train neither happy nor unhappy and got out at Euston and started the walk home. It was when I reached the Park I suddenly realized I was walking without my painting. Back I went to the station but it was never found. It was a snow scene – with a loneliness I know about, having been brought up in Burnley not far off. It had black factories and three figures, black like the factories. The sky was dark and like a grim threat. Although I never saw it again, I know it in detail – having that sort of memory, I guess. I ask you, what a thing, eh? Oh well, he has gone, bless him. I'm glad you wrote that thing about him.

The letter makes me feel there is more than one way of owning a picture. It tells a real story, by which I mean that though it actually did happen, it need not have done, since it's true anyway.

Getting Money for It

I got back from the trip to America and the first thing I heard was my girlfriend had left me, and I went right off my food. 'What about writing a bit of poetry about it?' my friend Atfield said, but I just sat in a corner and kept on thinking about it in case I forgot for a minute, and then had to go through the awful business of remembering.

I had an egg the fourth day and Atfield said to my mother, 'It's good to see him back on his vittles.' He was half way between thinking I'd been pretending and wondering whether four days was about par for this sort of thing. All I could tell him was you started out trying not to burst into tears all the time, and ended up feeling annoyed. And it was the annoyance that made this first piece anyone ever paid me for come out so nice and easy.

First I had a go at painting the garage doors, but I was held up by the casements round the little windows and got gloomy again. Then I raked out my two pairs of trousers and the sports-jacket and went at them with a clothes-brush, desperately trying to stifle the decay in their poor threads. But this induced a paroxysm of rage so melancholy that I stormed downstairs, accused my mother of being unable to cook risotto, and sat down fuming with paper and pencil.

What I had to do was write about America for the *Isis*. A bunch of us from the OUDS had spent the previous few weeks touring a couple of plays round the campuses of the Middle West and there hadn't been a dull moment. I squared up to the paper and kicked off in high *Isis* style, which at that period had taken a particularly nauseous and euphuistic turn (the object was to hit off a kind of runic idiom designed to make everyone who read it feel left out of something. I don't think I could give you a sample without blushing, it's like reading your old history essays, quite unbearable). Anyway, what with my feelings being so hot and concentrated, this *Isis* style of writing acted on me like the casements of the garage windows, a fearful bottleneck, and I gave a great yell, thumped the dining-room table and started to write it all down just as it came to me.

What the annoyance did was free me from any feelings that couldn't be immediately absorbed by the job in hand, it soaked up so much of me I didn't have time to be conditional: it didn't make me say things I didn't mean, it just let me say things I did mean as though they were the last word. Rather like being drunk. Not that I thought this at the time, I just wrote it and took it up with me when term started, gave it to the editor and went out into the streets of Oxford whistling the theme-song of the last film I'd seen with the girl, and whistling it very loud on the off-chance she might overhear.

When the article came out I was stopped in the street by a don I knew. 'You shouldn't have done it. Some of us are hoping to spend sabbaticals there and this sort of thing just doesn't help.' I moved on, startled. All I'd done was be a bit lofty. I'd made jokes about coke machines and launderettes (creatures from outer space, they were, in 1950), larded the piece with stuff about the Americans not being very good at thinking, pulled their legs about universities where you could get degrees in creative angling, and said the national drink was pink ice-cream in ginger-beer.

To my further amazement, the following Wednesday there was a page of letters complaining about the thing. 'Charles Dickens,' said the President of the Union, who happened to be an American, 'Matthew Arnold and Fanny Trollope have done it before, and they were clever.' I doubt if he envisaged the simple pleasure he would give me by letting me know I didn't deserve to be numbered among that company, though who Fanny Trollope was, if she wasn't the President's grandma, I couldn't think.

A Rhodes scholar said the article hadn't bothered him, he had barely mustered enough energy to dismiss it to his landlady as 'the broken narrow-bore quills of a very provincial porcupine'. I tried to imagine him rising on his elbow in his day-bed to deliver this throw-away line, but it couldn't be done, and as I read further in the correspondence – the pink ice-cream in ginger-beer appeared to be the real infuriator, perhaps because there was an occult exactness about it that I hadn't calculated – an unlovely smile stole across my face. I was no expert, but judging by the operatic nature of the response, I had hit some sort of target.

Better than I knew. The phone rang while I was in the *Isis* office receiving the congratulations of less fortunate scribes. It was *Time* magazine – could they print a picture of me? Stifling a desire to burst into tears of happiness, I said should I send them a snap. No, no, they'd take the picture themselves. I replaced the receiver with a petulant sigh – was one to be pestered night and day, was one to be given no peace? I stalked off in what should have been an awed silence but which was, in fact, a hail of bad language, envious slurs and rolled-up balls of paper.

The next day the photographer arrived, a nice tall thin man on the order of Mel Ferrer. He took about two hundred pictures of me smoking a cigarette. I don't know why I chose to be photographed smoking a cigarette, because after all I didn't smoke. All I can say is it seemed the right thing to do at the time.

I obeyed the photographer's every whim, nay I anticipated him. 'What about one looking sort of witty?' I cried, throwing myself back in the chair and curling the corner of my lip that hadn't got a fag lodged under it. Touched by this display of uninhibited narcissism, the photographer felt he had to tell me the truth: 'They aren't after an interesting picture,' he said, 'I think they just want a nasty one.'

Which they got. I came out looking like a dwarf caught in the middle of a fire-eating act. But I forgave them everything when I read the caption: 'Oxford's Robinson,' it said, just like that. I walked round the town trying to whistle, but every time I went to purse my lips I found I was grinning. They'd reprinted the article and this time the letters rolled in from all over the world. 'An essay in impertinence', 'Cockney insolence', 'Anyone who consents to having an article published by *Time* deserves having such a dreadful picture of himself published with it', 'his mental myopia'. *Time* printed a page of them, the *Isis* did a centre-spread, and the Waynflete Professor of Chemistry (at that time Sir Robert Robinson) received a lot of abusive letters not intended for him.

I was coming to recognize the sort of insult you only got when you'd really drawn blood, and I glowed when I read them. There was only one that slipped under my complacency – 'If he wears the crown of wit, let him watch it doesn't slide down over his ears' – because while we'd been doing these two plays in America that's exactly what a crown had done. I was sustaining the not absolutely central role of the Duke of Burgundy in King Lear, and the crown I was given wasn't a very good one. In fact, one night before we went on, it came apart, and I stuck it together with elastoplast.

Well, the Duke of Burgundy has to do a lot of standing about while

Lear is going on about Cordelia, and as I stood there I felt an ominous shifting in the region of the scalp and suddenly realized that the heat of my head was melting the elastoplast and the crown was settling lower and lower. I don't think for sheer naked impotence there's a situation to match standing on a stage with a crown sinking down towards your ears and knowing that the moment you move – a moment that is slowly getting nearer and nearer – it must inevitably fall off.

If it had been a hat I could have done something, but you can't take off a crown and fan yourself with it as though it was getting hot. 'Come, noble Burgundy,' thundered Lear, and the bloody thing slid past my ears and settled round my neck. I tell you, I used to wake up in the night thinking about that, and it lent the words of my hostile correspondent a surreal menace.

Well, that was more or less that, and I was sitting in my rooms in Bear Lane one night having another little read of the piece in *Time* and chuckling over what a bang-up success it had all been, when a thought struck me like a thunderclap: what about seeing if they'd pay me into the bargain! I sprang to the table and composed the letter and inside a week had received a cheque for six guineas. Fame, fortune, and – for all those who like a happy ending to be really happy – the girl as well. She sent me a clipping of the horrible *Time* picture with 'Gee, you look cosmopolitan' scribbled on the back. We spent that six guineas together, in a haze of love and delight.

Arm in Arm with Borges

I gave Borges my arm and we walked through the park at the top of the Avenida Marcelo T. d'Alvear. We walked very slowly for Borges is blind, and though he has been blind for more than twenty years he treads timidly, as people do who are not blind but close their eyes trying to imagine what it would be like. I was shoulder to shoulder with an oracle, for people ran up to Borges and put questions to him with the half-smiling faces they would wear when they told the story at home: 'I was in the park, and you know, I saw Borges – and I asked him, Borges why have you not committed suicide as you said you would in that article you wrote for the newspaper? And – you know what he replied? – Borges said, "You must not believe all you read."'

What looked like the entire population of Buenos Aires was on its knees repairing holes in the pavement in time for the World Cup, and of course there are some things which if they are not done for a silly reason are not done at all. A band of soldiers in lion-tamers' outfits were playing wind instruments, while a visiting general laid a wreath at the foot of a statue which, whatever it commemorated, was a monument to hysteria. There were real soldiers with single hairs sticking out of chins that had never yet seen a razor, patrolling in their jungle-greens at the periphery of the celebrations, aiming their machine-guns at the stomachs of passers-by. I had been reading aloud to Borges from Sir Thomas Browne, later exchanging with him a shout or two from *Beowulf*, and now I had some sense that time had fallen out of its conjugations just as it does in a Borges story, and everything that *had* happened, and everything that was going to happen, was taking place now – instantaneously. A man came up to Borges and asked him to remind him of the first line of *The Odyssey*, saying, 'It is so long since I composed the poem I have forgotten it.' Or so I dreamed.

But this is the Borges effect. A story by Borges swings like a bright glass in front of your eyes, and through it you may see the theologian Swedenborg dreaming that though he is dead he is unconscious of the fact: until, opening a familiar door in his own house, he finds, within, a tropical rain-forest. Or a man seduced by the daughter of the caretaker of a great house, waking one morning to the sound of hammers, and finding as he walks into the next room that the noise was produced by the carpentry necessary for his own crucifixion, which then takes place.

In Borges, the dreams dovetail, the geometry is reciprocal. Lying in his garden by a well, beneath a tree, in Cairo, a man dreams his fortune is to be found in Isfahan. But when he arrives in Isfahan he is beaten by the chief of police there, who abuses him for his credulity, telling him that *he* dreams that his own fortune is to be found by a well, beneath a tree, in a garden in Cairo, but he is not so foolish that he pays attention to dreams. The man returns to Cairo, and by his own well, in his own garden, beneath his own tree, he finds his treasure.

A bishop calls on a magician and pleads to be instructed in the magic art. The magus bids his maid prepare some partridges for supper, but gives her orders that she is not to cook them until he tells her. Then he says to the bishop that he fears great men are sparing of their favours once they have what they want, but the bishop assures him of his good will, and the magus instructs him. The bishop is made a cardinal, then becomes Pope, and all the time the magician follows in his train, waits upon his favour, but is treated peremptorily, and is at last dismissed. 'Will you at least give me food for the return journey?' he asks, but the pontiff brusquely refuses. 'Then,' says the magus, 'I must roast the partridges I ordered for supper.' Both bishop and magus stand once more in the magus's library: the moment has been suspended, no time has passed at all.

The glass swings in the fingers of a hypnotist, and readers of Borges – 'A good reader is rarer than a good writer,' Borges says – find the incidents of their actual lives moving into patterns that are distinctly Borgesian (Borges says of Kafka that Kafkaesque traces are to be found in Browning and Kierkegaard, but that these strains would have been unidentifiable had Kafka never existed). As I shuffle with Borges along the formal pathways that evoke those labyrinths in his stories which grow until they fill the universe, in this park which gives me the illusion that it transects time, as though it were a sepia photograph of long ago joining the moment it was taken to the moment I observe it, I begin to think of a picture that hangs on a wall at home.

It is a picture of a country house, painted in the seventeenth century by Samuel van Hoogstraten, and when I brought it home I wondered what it was that made me uneasy. Then I realized. The picture was not of the actual house, it was of the gatehouse. The house itself remained unpainted, save for a single column at the edge of the canvas, and I as the onlooker was standing inside it. Then one day, in a gallery in another country, I saw a second picture by Hoogstraten. A woman with a dog walked within the colonnade of a country house. She was looking in my direction, and this seemed natural, for the first column in her picture is missing – and it is the last column in mine. When I discover all the other pictures, and the house finally has its four walls, will I be able to find a door in the canvas and open it into the enormous face of Hoogstraten? And as his brush hovers over his palette, will he agree to let me out before he paints me, irrevocably, in?

I repeat: it is the Borges effect. His stories hang in the glass he swings before your eyes like the brightly lit moments of a consuming fever. And his poems, conjuring the suburbs of Buenos Aires, have so successfully dreamed the dream on everyone's behalf that when I ventured into Palermo, the outlying district of Borges's youth, with its cobbled streets, neglected pillarboxes, and abandoned tramlines, I felt I must have been born here too but had somehow forgotten my old address. Every opening door and narrow passageway, every rusty balcony with a singing-bird hanging in its cage, every secret courtyard, spoke of something familiar, and I could not tell if this were the furniture of a poem or of reality:

> The garden's grillework gate
> opens with the ease of a page
> in a much-thumbed book,
> and, once inside, our eyes
> have no need to dwell on objects
> already fixed and exact in memory.
> Here habits and minds and the private language
> all families invent
> are everyday things to me.
> What necessity is there to speak
> or pretend to be someone else?
> The whole house knows me,
> they're aware of my worries and weakness.
> This is the best that can happen –
> what Heaven will grant us:
> not to be wondered at or required to succeed
> but simply let in
> as part of an undeniable Reality
> like stones of the road, like trees.

That day I returned via the Recoleta Cemetery, where Borges looks forward with satisfaction to occupying the family tomb. The cemetery is a sort of Mayfair of the dead, the most expensive real estate in Buenos Aires, each sepulchre a wild confection of urns and angels, pediments and cupolas, an architecture of Babel on whose pinnacles stone generals are carried into Valhalla in full evening-dress. It was lunchtime when I arrived, and sharp black shadows lay across the paths as though the sun itself were carving the entablature, and workmen retired into the tombs to feast, spreading tablecloths on the coffins of their betters. But now in the park Borges said to me: 'About half an hour ago I felt sure I was about to die. I tried to become curious about the event, but I failed. I wanted only to get it over with.' We moved slowly across the road. Borges said: 'Perhaps half an hour ago, we both died, and very soon now we shall realize it.'

What Borges Said

When he was an adolescent, Borges began to re-invent Buenos Aires in his imagination.

J.L.B.: I think it began way back in 1914, when I was in Europe, in Switzerland: I began thinking about Buenos Aires and changing it, recasting it, remoulding it. I suppose I've greatly exaggerated things – that was up to me to do, being a writer. I knew the whole thing was more or less trumped up by me, but somehow I had to do it – yes, it's part of my homesickness.

R.R.: And when you returned here, did it seem strange?

J.L.B.: When I returned to it, I found it was quite unlike what I had been dreaming up all the time. It never existed really, but now it exists in my imagination and in many people's imagination. I'm an old man – they believe what I say.

⌒ Borges is a poet, but his best poems are stories – fictions that are like the torn edge of some other universe. To quote André Maurois, 'Borges has no spiritual homeland. He creates imaginary and symbolic worlds outside space and time.' Or perhaps from so far within space and time that his brief tales seem to come from some deeper-seated, older brain that remembers the monsters. They incorporate distortions of place and period and time and identity, but as in the dreams of a child who is delirious the contents of rooms are sinisterly enlarged or horribly diminished, the distortions feel authentic. As though it were possible that the world of which these fictions are a special reflection were itself a fiction – a world that belongs particularly to Borges.⌒

J.L.B.: Well, if you believe in Berkeley and idealism, then, of course, all things are fiction. I mean experience is a dream, there is no real difference between a working experience and a dreaming experience. And if you think of your own past life, then you think in terms of memory, and memory seems to be a fiction also. Every time we remember something we slightly change it, my father told me so.

R.R.: Have you always had this sense of what other people might call reality being a fiction or a dream?

J.L.B.: Well, I was brought up on idealism, so I suppose so. My father was a teacher of psychology and was very fond of metaphysics. As a child I was taught the Eleatic paradoxes without the name being mentioned. My father just taught me those paradoxes by using a chessboard after dinner. 'What is the colour of the orange?' I would very cleverly answer, 'Orange-coloured.' 'That doesn't carry us very far.' 'Well,' I would say, 'it is coloured, let's say, between red and yellow.' 'That's better. But in the dark, do you think it has that colour, what is the taste of the orange, do you think that the orange is tasting its own flavour all the time?' I was being led to ideas without my father mentioning the name of Berkeley or the name of the Eleatic. I was really taught all those things when I was a child.

R.R.: When did you first start to be a writer? How early in childhood?

J.L.B.: I always was a writer even before I began to write. I always thought of myself as being a writer. I was brought up in my father's library. I was reading and writing all the time – in fact, the first work I ever did was an attempt at a handbook on Greek mythology.

R.R.: It is a curious thing, is it not, to want to make things up, to invent stories, to make fantasies, write dreams?

J.L.B.: Yes, but in my case I should say it is a habit. When I'm alone, when I'm by myself, I try to concoct stories, to begin poems. It seems to me that literature is my life work – you know, I mean I keep on at it.

R.R.: Has your blindness been part of the creative process?

J.L.B.: Yes, it has, it has made me work the more, think the more, dream the more. I think blindness may be quite useful to a man of letters. It makes him stick to his job.

R.R.: Has it altered your perception of favourite objects at all?

J.L.B.: Well, of course, when I look at my friends I think of them in the terms of how their faces were when I went blind. I look at a friend of mine and I know the way he or she looks, and I think of 1955 or

1950-odd – I haven't seen them since then. I don't know what my own face is like. It may be awful, for all I know – or it may have bettered.

R.R.: That reminds me of an image in one of your stories. I was thinking of the man who had thought he would assemble the universe on a wall, and he found once he'd done that, it was his own face.

J.L.B.: I think that's a true parable, no? That's what every writer does. In the case of Byron, for example. I don't think of his work – not even of *Don Juan*. We think of Byron himself, so that all his work has gone to the making of his face. It was the case of Carlyle, also. In the case of Dickens, no – because Dickens is lost in the crowd of his characters. So is Shakespeare, of course, you don't think of them as individuals.

R.R.: Could you, do you think, reading your own words, construe yourself from them?

J.L.B.: I suppose I could, but I'd have to read them and I can't very well do that – I'd be bored stiff.

R.R.: But if they were read to you?

J.L.B.: I wouldn't like the experience. And yet now and then I come on a really fine sonnet, and then I say, 'How on earth did I write it?' I enjoy, somehow, my own verse – my own prose I can't stand. My own verse comes back to me: I know many verses by heart. I can intone them and sometimes I feel quite jealous of the man who wrote them, feel I am quite unworthy to have written them.

R.R.: You've said that you're not a fabulist or a preacher of parables.

J.L.B.: I am not. You would hardly call me Aesop. Besides, I wonder if my opinions are important. I suppose that, for my literary purpose, opinions are unimportant. What a writer wants to do is not what he does. I think that Kipling wrote that it might be given to a writer to invent a fable, but not to know what the fable stood for – that was not granted him.

R.R.: You've described the process of writing as a guided dream.

J.L.B.: A guided dream, yes. I seem to be seeing something a long way off, let's say an island, and I can make out both ends, I mean the end and the beginning. But what I can't make out is what's there in between. That I have to discover by myself or invent for myself. Then, when I have the beginning of a story and the end of a story, I have to find out whether that story happened let's say at the turn of the century, or in some dim Eastern land, or in England for all I know – all those things are up to me.

⟋A striking figure in Borges's work is the labyrinth. The world in his stories is an enclosure of forking paths and formal gardens, endlessly recurring galleries in libraries that fill the universe, an architecture of Babel in which one room is the mirror image of the next, a geometry which continuously expands to obliterate space itself.⟍

J.L.B.: Well, of course, it stands for perplexity. It's a very obvious statement for being baffled. I seem to be baffled all the time, not to understand the world I'm living in, so I fall back on the labyrinth as the most obvious symbol of perplexity. The English word 'maze' isn't as good as the word 'labyrinth' – you think of that enormous building whose heart is the Minotaur.

R.R.: Another feature – but a more external feature – of your writing is its brevity.

J.L.B.: Well, you see. I'm a very lazy man, that's a cause. Another cause is the fact that since I can't write personally, I have to dictate my story. That makes for brevity, also. And then if I think of a long narrative, I don't really see it, it has to be successive. Whereas in the case of a short story, or, even more, of a short poem, I think that I can see it at a glance – it's my own, really. I'm very fond of short stories and I don't think I am really fond of novels, except, of course, the great examples. I suppose my chief English example will be Joseph Conrad.

R.R.: Have you ever been tempted to write a novel?

J.L.B.: No. Hardly ever been tempted to read a novel if it comes to that. As for Tolstoy and Dostoevsky, I liked them when I was a young man and now I don't. I can't stand them. Of course, taste changes.

⟋Borges the man is distinguished by a transcending gentleness of manner, a diffidence, a timidity even, which makes a notable contrast with the violent nature of certain of his stories. In his pages, flamboyant ruffians – real or imagined – engage in duels fought with coldness and ferocity, in which the invariable weapon is the knife. But why?⟍

J.L.B.: Because I seem to be homesick for violence, since my forefathers were military men and I have led a very quiet life myself. I suppose that will be the reason. Besides, the fact is that our history is very new. The war of independence, Rosas's dictatorship, the civil wars, the winning of the west or the conquering of the desert, as we call it – these things are near to me. I've been hearing of them all my life. I feel rather sorry for myself. My life is rather a sedentary life, a quiet life.

R.R.: And the knife is another image.

J.L.B.: The knife, at least in my time in this country, stood for personal courage, when in England, of course, you think of a knife as being something perfidious.

R.R.: Yes, that's true.

J.L.B.: But here, when you think of a knife, you think in terms of a knife duel, and then you have to be a brave man.

Borges has been honoured in England, but his attachment to England seems a natural consequence of his English forebears – his grandmother on his father's side was called Haslam and had come out to Argentina from Burslem in Staffordshire. To Borges, English literature is pre-eminent.

J.L.B.: I think of English literature as being *the* literature and of English as being *the* language, because in the case of German, another language I greatly love, you only have Teutonic words while in English you have both Latin and Saxon words.

R.R.: Do you find Shakespeare is the figure who sums up the Englishness of English literature for you?

J.L.B.: No, I don't think of Shakespeare as being – forgive my heresy – particularly English. He never went in for understatement. For example, I think of Wordsworth as being far more of an English poet. But perhaps every nation chooses somebody as its spokesman far away from itself. For example, Goethe is hardly a typical German. Cervantes is hardly a typical Spaniard. Cervantes is full of irony, of tolerance – and, well, he was a contemporary of the Inquisition.

Borges's reading is comprehensive, not surprisingly since he once made his living as a librarian, and it was, indeed, a bitter irony that he should have been made Director of the National Library at much the same time that his blindness became total. In the fifties, he was appointed Professor of English and North American studies in the University of Buenos Aires. This brings me to his interest in Old English, Anglo-Saxon.

J.L.B.: Somehow I thought I wanted to go back to my forefathers in England, and they may have been Saxon, for all I know. I remember

the first sentence I ever read in Old English, and I was intoxicated
with those words.

⌒Borges's mother died at the age of ninety-nine, and there is no
doubt he feels bewildered without her – she was his secretary,
amanuensis, travelling companion. Borges is himself much possessed
by death, and finds consolation in the prospect of it.⌒

J.L.B.: I hope to die wholly. I mean I hope to die body and soul, you
know. And yet there should be a meaning to life, though I don't think
it can be granted to us to know it. I don't believe in God either. When
I feel worried, when I feel wretched, I always find a consolation in
the thought that all this will very soon be over, I shall die and I shall
be utterly forgotten, I shall forget myself, which is the same thing. I
only think of death as a great hope, a hope of nothingness – but really
a great hope, and it really helps me to think of death as nothingness.

⌒Borges will sometimes pass off real characters as imagined, and
imagined ones as real. He has a taste for the literary practical joke,
the invention of oeuvres that couldn't have existed – Pierre Menard,
for instance, a twentieth-century author who undertook to compose
Don Quixote, word for word, without reference to the original.⌒

J.L.B.: That was my first venture into fiction, the first short story I
ever wrote. Of course, it's a hoax, it was not meant to be taken other
than as a hoax. I suppose perhaps he thought: 'Well, there are far too
many books in the world, the only thing to do is to rewrite the old
ones.' That may be an explanation. Really, I wrote that story so long
ago that I can't explain it.

⌒Borges says that he would like to be remembered by a single work,
a brief passage of prose he calls 'Borges and I' – it is a true reflection
on the seriality of his vision, in which he speaks of himself as though
he were not one man but two.⌒

Borges and I

The other one, the one called Borges, is the one things happen to. I walk
through the streets of Buenos Aires and stop for a moment, perhaps mechanically now, to look at the arch of an entrance hall and the grillework on the
gate; I know of Borges from the mail and see his name on a list of professors
or in a biographical dictionary. I like hourglasses, maps, 18th-century

typography, the taste of coffee and the prose of Stevenson; he shares these preferences, but in a vain way that turns them into the attributes of an actor. It would be an exaggeration to say that ours is a hostile relationship. I live, let myself go on living, so that Borges may contrive his literature, and this literature justifies me.

Years ago I tried to free myself from him and went from the mythologies of the suburbs to the games with time and infinity, but those games belong to Borges now and I shall have to imagine other things. Thus my life is a fight and I lose everything and everything belongs to oblivion, or to him. I do not know which of us has written this page.

High Life

I had to hire a suit of tails for the Lord Mayor's Midsummer Banquet. Tails are OK for tall thin snooty people, but all they do for the rest of us is exaggerate our deficiencies. Putting on a suit of tails, I feel that I am already wearing a surgical boot which I am carefully whitewashing so that it will show up better. By the time the man who was kitting me out had said, 'Don't pay any attention to the label, sir,' and I'd looked at the tab inside the collar and saw that it read 'Portly', I realized the evening was already ruined. On the actual night I was so disappointed with the figure I cut in the bathroom mirror – I looked like an ill-conditioned bouncer – I started to shout with rage, and I worked up such a lather that all the starch ran out of the collar of the shirt before we left the house. I sailed steaming into the Mansion House, and somehow I hadn't done up those little tabs on the bottom of the shirt and the white waistcoat that keep the whole lot anchored to the trousers, so it was all riding up, and I was shaking hands with the Lord Mayor with one hand while holding the other elegantly across my middle as though us swells always walked around like that.

I was so angry I was ready to explode, and it's funny when you're disappointed with yourself you somehow contrive your own downfall, which is literally what I did. As I stormed off to collar a couple of glasses of champagne, teeth chattering with self-hatred, I managed to get my foot into one of those big copper fish-kettles they put on the floor as ashtrays, and I thundered to the floor. My wife, who was

talking to some people, said she saw my big maddened red face and
then suddenly it disappeared and she heard this terrible rumble as I
hit the parquet, and a waiter came over – I thought to give me a hand
– but as I looked up at him from the floor through the starred lenses
of my broken glasses, he said, 'Would you be kind enough to give me
your autograph for my small daughter?'

Now Hear This

A correspondent from Kidderminster sent me an anthro-
pological curio. Enclosing the specimen, he wondered if I had ever
seen such a thing before, and admitted he passed it to me out of
sensations of ungovernable rage. 'Indeed,' he wrote, 'in quieter
moments I am appalled at the strength and spontaneity of my
reaction.' He went on to say that in making the object available to
me he had no feelings of guilt that perhaps he was breaching any
unwritten law of politeness or confidentiality, since the writer
evidently wished it to have the widest possible circulation.

It was a letter – or more properly, a circular – issued by a family,
and crammed with information about themselves. But as my correspondent savagely notes (he receives a number of these duplicated
news-sheets at Christmas time), 'the bulletins only include success
stories. Whereas George's promotion and Caroline's A-levels are
prominently featured, no mention is made of George losing his licence,
or Caroline helping the police with their inquiries.' In short, it is a
family commercial, and the example I was given went as follows:

Dear All – Sending this out in a bit of a rush since Eric and I are preparing
for our trip to China. Shanghai, Peking and the Wall are all on the itinerary,
and we're taking no chances, clothing-wise (our wonderful month in North
Dakota – did I tell you? – taught us a thing or two about dressing for the
occasion). How different from Madeira it's all going to seem – we had a
gorgeous time there in the spring, and Deirdre's Spanish improved wonderfully. It was a much needed *break*, as Eric had been working non-stop since
his appointment as sales director of the Loamshire Fodder Mills, and what
with moving to a new house (ravishing views, but landscaping six acres can
be a headache!) we felt ready for a little pampering.

Deirdre has turned into quite a little gymnast and has represented the school on the parallel bars, while Douglas's nose is still in his books – the headmaster feels he's scholarship material, and he's now grappling with the sort of physics that even Eric, with his B.Sc., finds testing. It's a wee bit isolated here, and Eric's chauffeur has been a pet, ferrying the children to and from school, in between carrying the lord and master to board meetings.

Jinny, the tortoiseshell, had six kittens, and Rug, our darling Old English Sheepdog, stands guard over them just like Nanna in *Peter Pan*. All in all, life's very hectic, but *very* satisfying, and we wish all our friends as happy and successful a year as we've just enjoyed ourselves …

'It's just possible,' adds my Kidderminster correspondent, 'that my distress arises from the fact that neither I nor any member of my family seems to have done anything remotely worth bringing to public attention in this way. But if we ever did do anything spectacular – perhaps going to Clacton for the day, or winning a toffee-apple at a fair – I hope we would resist this kind of indecent exposure.

'Oh, just before I finish,' he concludes, 'the only nice thing about the round robin I sent you is the information that Deirdre's Spanish improved wonderfully during their holiday in Madeira. Since they all speak Portuguese on that island, she must have worked like a beaver.'

Priestley

One Sunday I opened the colour supplement and saw J. B. Priestley sitting there, and I knew I was looking at a trespasser. Colour supplements are full of faces whose features seem to have been stamped on them through a dozen thicknesses of carbon-paper, the faces of people in advertisements, so standardized that if one of them stabbed you to the heart, you'd have difficulty identifying him to the police. And here, amid all the non-entity that was blowing like a gale through the After Eight mint, was the presence of a real live human being. So irreducibly himself, so utterly his own man, that the advertisers – who use colour supplements as a hall of mirrors in which they hope we will find ourselves distorted into consumers – the advertisers must have felt betrayed: J. B. Priestley is too identifiable to be identified with.

He was smiling politely in the picture, no doubt grateful that the whim of the photographer had extended only as far as planting him among his own rhododendrons, and not on the roof, say, of King's College Chapel. But amid all those magazine faces, faces glowing with the pride of having obediently *bought* something, faces that looked exactly the part only because they were acting it – there was Priestley, not the image, but the reality.

I suppose if you wanted someone who *looked* right for a writer, you might not hire Priestley. Sometimes his face can take on the faintly threatening aspect of a man in an oil-shop profoundly dubious of selling anyone a pound of nails, and this of course would unfit him for the modelling job. But then writers who look too much like writers may have to spend as much time doing the looking as doing the writing, and I relished the contrast – as I've often relished the contrast – between Priestley and the Image Men.

As he's said himself, he's not spent five minutes of his writing life considering what an audience might like. He's considered what *he* might like, then declared it. This way of doing it (where a writer dares to identify himself) isn't half as fashionable as the other way of doing it – where a writer waits for the *audience* to identify him, to construct him in their own image and, after he's supplied whatever it is they bespeak, to hang him up in the broom cupboard until the next time they want their prejudices massaged. Writers and performers in this age of mass media are highly prized and highly paid in so far as they are able to put an audience on good terms with itself by never obtruding themselves. But Priestley has always taken the risk. He does obtrude himself. As author or pamphleteer, playwright, essayist or talker, he's always been present, he's been there in the room, he's been there to be counted.

His method is to respond, not to calculate. And at a time when fiction becomes faction (a warm-up of the merely factual, a compiler's job, a paste-up from a card-index of guaranteed preoccupations – a way, really, of defacing reality by scribbling on it), at such a time Priestley still does it the magic way. He scrutinizes closely – and then he guesses. And at the top of his bent, in a novel like *Bright Day* or *Lost Empires*, in plays like *Time and the Conways* or *Johnson Over Jordan*, his guesses amount to divination. He brings us together – not like the

Image Men in order to sell us something, not in order coldly to exploit our weaknesses rather than warmly to gratify our desires – but at the level where men and women are truly joined, the level where the dreams are dreamt, Priestley broaches the reader's own dream, by broaching his own. And he gives us what only the rare ones give us: a sense that we are collaborating, rather than simply paying to go in. He admits us to the country of ourselves.

This might sound solemn, and that would be a poor compliment to Priestley. Serious he is, but solemnity isn't his ticket. You've only to hear the relish with which he tells you about the chap on the *TV Times* who rang him up and asked him (the most widely read author in the English language) to do a profile of Mike and Bernie Winters and, as an added inducement to get him to do it, explained that it would be a profile *in depth*. Or you might see him gravely nod as someone advances the merits of educational cruises, commenting – with equal gravity – that he supposed it kept them out of the public houses. Solemnity is not his line.

What I've been trying to single out is the quality I think I honour in Priestley above all others – the sense he gives me of inviolable identity. At a time when there are so many salesmen, all of them intent, whether in politics or in communications, on melting the individual down, the better to sell him something – at such a time we do ourselves a favour if we celebrate a man who has never peddled anything to anyone in his life. A man who fits no trend, nor wishes to, whose work has not only fleeted the hours for many (as he once said he hoped it had) but is able to do more. Is able to startle us into knowing, over and over again, that individuality is something that must neither be surrendered nor hoarded.

I once went to dine in a restaurant with Priestley, and the waiter asked him, 'Have you a reservation?' And I remember thinking, as the mundaneness of the situation seemed just for a second to be transcended, that – No, he has no reservation: but in the roll-call of time he will turn out to have had something rather better, he will turn out to have been among the founders of the feast.

Ferret-proof

I saw a pair of stout knickerbockers in a shop in Oxford, and the ticket pinned to them said they were guaranteed by the Country Gentleman's Association, or some such name, and underneath that it said 'Ferret-proof'. I wondered how the point was established. I concluded it must be carried out, under conditions of scientific rigour and strict control, at ferret-proofing grounds, probably just south of Bicester. A handpicked member of *Burke's Landed Gentry* is buttoned into the knickerbockers – 'Whenever you're ready, m'lord' – 'Very well, Thomas, let the little beggars out.' And a sackful of ferrets tumble over each other, giving their characteristic high mewing cry – sure sign they have sighted a pair of knickerbockers – and once more, hope undiminished by experience, they attempt for the umpteenth time the impossible penetration, and for the umpteenth time the buckles frustrate them. 'I think that puts it beyond dispute, eh, Thomas?' And the coveted certificate is (like those seals of efficiency handed out to Swiss watches) reluctantly conceded.

Sir Ralph Rehearses

In the morning about ten o'clock, the insides of theatres smell like tombs. All those evenings at eight, all that old fun, turned to dust.

'Is Jimmy there? What about Lancelot's opening speech? I think we ought to get on.'

Mr Glen Byam Shaw sat in the middle of the Theatre Royal, Haymarket, and all the empty seats made him look like a man in a pocket-cartoon that was waiting for a caption.

'Jimmy? Would you like to do Lancelot's opening speech?'

'Not particularly,' said Jimmy with great sincerity, 'no.'

'Ye-e-e-es,' Mr Byam Shaw nodded, as though he wouldn't feel like doing it either if he were Jimmy, 'ye-e-e-es. Get Jessica, and we'll do the other bit.'

You could just hear the traffic outside. Bang, bang, went someone with a hammer.

'Can we have hush?'

'No you can't,' shouted a savage voice, off.

Jessica tripped on, wrapping an old red curtain round her waist to get her used to the long dress. She did a scene with Jimmy.

'It may sound silly,' Jimmy said across the footlights to the director, 'but if she holds the money back when she gives me the present, I just don't feel like weeping. You know?'

'Ye-e-e-es,' said Mr Byam Shaw, as though what Jimmy had said had told him volumes. 'Perhaps the holding it back is more of a joke, do you think?'

Jessica said her bit too quietly.

'Ah-oh-yes-yes-yes-,' she nodded in a passion of agreement when the director pointed it out. 'Yes-yes-.' She concentrated vehemently, not wanting to miss a word, focused herself on him as though he were telling her fortune.

'It's just – it's just that it's so terribly difficult when she's supposed to be whispering anyway –' she smiled apologetically, entering the teeniest caveat in the world.

'Ye-e-e-es,' said Mr Byam Shaw. 'I know, my love, but that's the art of it, isn't it?'

The dead smells of the early morning theatre perked up. Someone was smoking a pipe in the aisle. It was Sir Ralph.

'Ted,' called Mr Byam Shaw, 'are you worried?'

'Yes.'

'Why?'

'I don't know.'

Sir Ralph spoke to Mr Byam Shaw, who nodded. 'Ted,' he shouted. 'Sir says why don't you raise your hat to the pole? It would make it funnier.'

When the actors were advised by the director, they telegraphed intense interest. As though light were breaking through, almost unbearably. There was a great climate of politeness, as though nobody wanted to be the least trouble to anybody else.

'Be careful, Paul,' warned Mr Byam Shaw, 'you are emotionally leaning forward. Let the author speak.'

Sir Ralph sailed up the proscenium steps, slipped into a white lumber-jacket, removed his glasses with a discovering flourish, and acted everyone out of the window.

'Let us have the lantern lit –' it sounded like a marvellous line, but he was only making a suggestion – 'Is there anything more dull than a black lantern – eh? It need not be ela-bor-ate.'

'Don't shamble off, boys, act off,' said the director.

No shambling for Sir Ralph. All great actors are slightly duck-footed (a natural subject for a D.Phil.), it helps them get majesty into their legs. Sir Ralph moved off the stage on legs that might have been the royal yacht *Britannia*. When he came back, he said to Jessica. 'It would be awfully sweet if you went up on your toes to kiss my cheek.'

Jessica said, 'Oh dear, I was on my toes. I'm too small.'

'No,' said Sir Ralph, 'it is I who am too tall.'

An education to see him hand the keys to Jessica – 'Fast bind, fast find, A proverb never stale in thrifty mind' – winding the key-chain into her palm on every syllable, not as a calculated bit of business, but as a spontaneous earnest that he was Shylock. He couldn't not have done it.

'Talk to him, darling,' said Mr Byam Shaw to Portia, 'talk to him – don't spout. What are you bringing the brief on for?'

'Well, I won't bring the brief on if it worries you,' Portia, who was very beautiful, said.

'It's just that the audience will be wondering what you've got it for, and I want them to be concentrating on you, you see.'

Sir Ralph said, 'I think it would be better if he shook the hand after the speech –'

'Yes, yes, quite.'

'Don't you think?'

'Oh yes, I do.'

Nerissa looked very nice in a very short mini-skirt. 'They're all acting away down there,' she said impishly, 'and I'm left up here.' She did a sorry-for-herself face, but comically, in case anyone thought she really was.

'Poor Nerissa feels miserably left out,' said Mr Byam Shaw thoughtfully.

'You see, I'm stuck behind him.'

'Ah,' said Mr Byam Shaw, 'well, darling, why not look over his shoulder?'

Sir Ralph was sharpening the knife on the sole of his beautifully polished brown shoes. 'It's a good knife, an excellent knife,' he told a lady with grey hair, who seemed very pleased to hear it.

'I don't want you to stand too tightly, boys, the audience mustn't be excluded,' said the director, stopping them. When they were interrupted, the actors felt themselves slightly encumbered by the bit of acting they'd just been doing, and tended to convert it into a funny walk.

Sir Ralph approached the footlights and peered into the darkness, shading his eyes with the splendid knife. 'Oh sir,' he called to somebody in the auditorium, 'you did not by chance remove a brown trilby hat in mistake for your own?'

The answer was no.

'Ah, ah,' cried Sir Ralph, in some anguish, 'you were My Only Hope.' He moved slowly off the stage, and the curtain came down for lunch.

Our Betters

In 1950, royal asides at public functions were printed in newspapers with the verbal elisions carefully subbed out. No royal person was allowed to say 'that's' or 'it's', they were always heard to speak the words in full. So that when – during his visit to the South Bank Exhibition – the King was handed a weather report which rather unnecessarily pointed out that it was raining, the *News Chronicle* got him down as saying, 'That Is Certainly Accurate.' On the same occasion, the Queen ('fascinated immediately by the 74-inch telescope') was heard – at least by the *Chronicle* man – to remark, 'What A Pity It Is Not Working.'

The words are recorded as though they aren't examples of speech so much as plucky imitations of it. Royalty has to talk (so the *Chronicle*'s message seems to go) because that's the primitive way you and I do it: left to themselves, they'd probably communicate by osmosis (an extension of the myth, rife among schoolboys, that the King and Queen never engaged in sexual congress, but produced children by methods that were very much more polite). But just because, by a wild act of graciousness, not to mention ventriloquial skill, they managed to adapt to our style, this was no excuse for listening too closely and overhearing those touches of the vernacular which might make a decent person feel he had startled his father by coming across him too suddenly in the lavatory.

The obligation felt by sub-editors to preserve this kind of distance, while at the same time pretending it was all going down verbatim, led to the concoction of royal ad libs that sounded as if they were being delivered over the public address system at a railway station. When Queen Elizabeth copped a deserter who had had the bad luck to stray into her bathroom at Windsor Castle, the *Sunday Pictorial* told its 1950 readers that she said, 'What Are You Doing Here?' and in case they missed the point, added that she said it 'without losing the natural poise and dignity associated with her' (an MVO, one might have thought, for the amanuensis hiding behind the door). Having got him nicely in her sights, the Queen (according to the *Pic*) then sent the following impromptu ringing round the white tile: 'And now I will press this bell and have you turned over to the Castle guard. I advise you to serve your punishment like a man – and then serve your country like one.' A clear case (if you took the *Pic*'s account literally) of a malefactor being cornered by a Speak-Your-Weight machine.

Perhaps the style was set by the royal speech writers. In 1950, it was still mandatory on royal persons to make statements that could be guaranteed to yield no meaning. 'When you leave school,' Princess Margaret was heard to say at a 1950 Speech Day, 'you will all go your different ways. But I know that each one of you will give something towards upholding and cherishing the great traditions which you have inherited.' It was a strange runic idiom, bearing little relation to human speech. Indeed, it was anti-speech, since its object was to insulate the speaker against the possibility of communication. 'Free men everywhere,' Princess Elizabeth discovered to President Truman on arrival at Idlewild, 'look towards the United States with affection and with hope. The message which has gone out from this great capital has brought help and courage to a troubled world.' But on this occasion the distinction between royal rhubarb and ordinary words was splendidly highlighted by the President's reply: 'I thank you, dear.'

There was no hint of discrimination in the reporting of royal 'news'. In 1950, the *Daily Mail* found space to tell its readers that Prince Charles had changed his parting ('from left to right'), and the *News Chronicle* revealed that the King owned two tartan dinner-jackets. 'For some time he has kept them a close secret,' the *Chronicle* added importantly, in case you hadn't realized it was a scoop. Pressed to say more, the tailor who had made these interesting garments was alleged to have replied, 'My lips are sealed.' A solemn aldermanic note was maintained, no doubt because the subs sensed that if the obligation to keep his face straight wasn't placed squarely on the reader, he might make a rude noise. 'News of a carefully kept secret was given at a distinguished gathering at London's Savoy Hotel last night. Princess Anne has been enrolled by the Automobile Association as its millionth member.' By making it perfectly clear that this information was to be judged not by profane but by sacred standards, the *Mail* was hoping to distract the reader from any suspicion that – since Princess Anne was only two months old – the Automobile Association may have slipped its cogs.

No discrimination, no irony. When Queen Juliana and Prince Bernhard gave a dinner for the King and Queen at Claridge's, fifty boxes of gold plate were sent on from Holland, along with seven chefs, one Master of the Royal House, two silver-room staff, two under-florists and a wardrobe man – an advance party later reinforced by thirty-one Dutch waiters, a clutch of footmen, and the royal florist. Three thousand freshly cut flowers were flown in, and the meal began with pâté de fois gras, turtle soup, went on to sole and capon, and ended with iced meringue and fruit. To drink, there were four several wines. At the time these events were being placed on record, a number of papers were carrying an advertisement for a dish called Brown Betty, a sinister compound conjured (in those days of austerity) from Weetabix and marmalade, and this ad could sometimes be seen flanked by another urging you to lay hands on a bottle of Rajah pickle 'and pep up your cheese sandwiches'.

Even so, the *News Chronicle* – culturally the most progressive of the popular dailies – made obeisance to the vulgarity of the Dutch state visit as though it had been Mr Pecksniff himself. The paper went so far as to print (with every sign of endorsing its premises) a hand-out prepared for the occasion by Claridge's Hotel: 'Reporters meet very polite but very complete barriers between them and people they want to see, and after wasting some time generally go quietly away, infected by the spirit of quiet good manners that abounds at Claridge's.' Purified by his contact with the hotel staff, the *Chronicle* man went down to Victoria where amid the loyal huzzas of the taxpayers, one royal family met the other. 'This moment,' reported the *Chronicle* man, still reeling from the cleansing influence of Claridge's, 'had all the warmth of delighted friends saying: "It's lovely to see you."' And manfully banishing from his recollection the fifty cases of gold plate and the thirty-one waiters, the reporter – a credit to hotel diplomacy, if ever there was one – added: 'The Queen and her Prince are such a homely couple.'

Having it both ways was a feature of royal reporting in 1950. The *Mirror* wanted to make it clear, or clearish, that although Princess Margaret had been known to buy a new dress, 'ball gowns are retrimmed and renovated, and so are hats'. Just in case you thought royalty was mostly engaged in the exhausting business of having a damn good time, the papers liked to draw your attention to homely economies. For instance, the Yeomen of the Guard: 'As the Yeomen retired,' reported the *Mail*, 'the King simply could not afford to replace them. There should be 100 Yeomen – now there are only 76.' Dashing a suspicious moisture from his eye, the 1950 reader was only too pleased to learn that 'the £40,000 the Yeomen and the Gentlemen-at-Arms cost will be met by the government'.

In case, from time to time, a subscriber was besieged by the thought that the business of waiting on royalty was anything other than an enviable pastime, magazines like *Woman* were alert to disabuse him: 'I often think,' wrote a correspondent in 1950, 'what fun it must be to be on the staff of Buckingham Palace. How proud you'd be to think if it wasn't for you, Princess Margaret wouldn't have had that boiled egg.' And the task of convincing the readership that royalty was having a hard time of it was intimately associated with that other branch of double-think, the proposition that if they hadn't devoted themselves to opening bazaars, they might well have soared to the top of any profession you cared to name. The *Chronicle* man's line on the Queen's visit to the South Bank — 'She was instantly fascinated by the 74-inch telescope' – is a little classic in this vein. Here, the reporter hints at a natural aptitude for astronomy that would have left Galileo standing at the gate.

In 1950, any indication that royalty wasn't wound up like clockwork was greeted by Fleet Street with open-mouthed incredulity. This was due both to a natural commercial disinclination to let an easy source of copy evaporate too quickly, and to a dull conviction that the readers shared the social prejudices of their scribes (it is as true now as it was then that the longest-lived editor is the one least distinguishable from his average reader). The *News Chronicle*, in attendance at the birth of Prince Charles, swore public fealty to what the subs secretly believed in, when it announced that 'a ghillie carried the good news to the King'. And borrowing a hazel-twig from the news editor, the *Chronicle* man divined that to the crowd outside Clarence House 'the birth of a royal baby is a needed symbol of national stability in an uncertain world'. This left the *Times* leader-writer free to strike a note of arcane bonhomie in allowing that 'as a future sovereign, Prince Charles may now look forward to exercising himself in the art of government at the head of his own nursery'. It was as though the newspaper-and-radio age of 1950 thought communications was a picture you looked at, instead of a window you looked through. How else account for the fact that when the *Mail* reported that Princess Margaret had been ticked off by Queen Mary for wearing a head-scarf and the old Queen had said, 'You look like a housemaid,' the *Mail* seemed to accept her premise, without at all convincing you it had noticed the implication.

The Place of the Volvo in Old Norse Mythology

I've always felt it was the car which went down to the showroom to choose the man, not the other way round, and Volvos like to pick a dentist who is going to send his son to a not quite first-rate public school. Never forget that Volvos come from the far north, and as each one rolls off the assembly-line it is ritually danced round by Lapland witches. Possibly this is why the front of a Volvo comes to look like the back of any other car, so that it appears to be travelling in a permanent state of reverse. And as you know, every Volvo driver takes a great oath, sworn before a notary public, never to turn his sidelights off – they are to be kept meaninglessly, mindlessly on at all times, in order to induce fury in other road-users. The lights, of course, don't radiate actual light, they radiate self-satisfaction, as though the driver is taking extra special care about some mysterious hazard – possibly reindeer or elk – that the rest of us are too thoughtless to bother about.

I'm a liberal in all this, of course, and I'd never supposed that Volvo owners were actually insane until I spoke to an expectant one – he was waiting for his new model, due to be flown in on a flight of broomsticks from Uppsala. 'Look,' he said, his eyes burning like sidelights, 'look – it's got a double brake-line and a treble oil-line, so you could take an axe' – he mimed this bit with an early edition of the *Evening Standard* – 'you could take an axe and actually sever' – saying 'sever', he drew back with his rolled-up paper and tipped three toilet-rolls out of the string-bag he was carrying over the same arm – 'you could sever one of the brake-lines or two of the oil-lines, and you'd still be laughing.' I said, 'What axe?' He said, 'What do you mean, what axe?' I said, 'The one you were talking about.' He said, 'No, no, I was just asking you to imagine.' Then he drew a deep breath as though he realized I wasn't up to this sort of intellectual rigour, and he said, 'There's even a little door on the headlights.' I said, 'Is that where the dwarf lives who works the windscreen-wipers?' 'Yes,' he said, 'and you only have to change his oil every 10,000 miles.'

What a Terrible State of Affairs There Appears to be in India

Books of advice live a life of their own. 'A drop of vinegar will loosen any screw.' Oh no, it won't! 'Keep spare safety-pins on a loop made with a pipe-cleaner.' Why? 'Clean behind radiators with a sponge-head dish-mop spliced onto a bamboo cane.' To what night-school do you go, and for how long, to learn the art of splicing? 'Strain lumpy paint through old nylon tights.' Then dance round it.

This absolutist strain was characteristic of the genre from the word go. 'Avoid making too much tea,' said the advice column in a nineteenth-century copy of the *Girls' Own Paper*, 'but when you have any over, give it, tea-leaves and all, to some poor person.' Walk out into the street, select a poor person, and let them have it (tea-leaves and all) straight up the snoot.

I have been familiar with this fatuously knowing tone ever since I came across an 1870 edition of *Inquire Within About Everything* in a disused fibre suitcase that nestled under the stairs next to our Goblin vacuum cleaner when I was about twelve. The bit I liked best was the section which gave instructions to a wife who wanted to brighten her husband's life by seeming to be his intellectual equal (seeming being the word, since the book tackled the whole problem as though it were an exercise in *travestie*). She was to bone up on the newspapers while he was away at the office, and when he got back in the evening, hot and peckish for his savoury marrow, she was to wait until he had seated himself behind the epergne, and then open the bowling with the words, 'My dear, what a terrible state of affairs there appears to be in India.' How the husband reacted when offered this apostrophe – like a year's supply of hair down a bathroom plug-hole, it would choke the most determined flow – is hard to imagine. Perhaps he retired to the conservatory, there to compose a telegram to a reliable alienist. But however disobliging his response, the wife was to say nothing: 'Let not a woman be tempted to utter anything sarcastic or violent. The bitterest repentance must needs follow if she do.' Ah, what care for the subjunctive, if not for the rights of women, they had in those days.

The smallest circumstance was taken to be a towering cliff-edge on which the whole world teetered. Hair dye, for instance – did it send you insane? 'A friend of ours,' avers *Inquire Within*, 'to whom we applied on the subject, favoured us with the following information: "I have operated upon my own cranium for at least a dozen years, and though I have heard it affirmed that dyeing the hair will produce insanity, I have the testimony of disinterested acquaintance that in my own case this principle cannot hold." ' Daftness was extended in all directions. 'Never meddle with gunpowder by candlelight,' said the columnist briskly, as though this were almost as common a cause of sudden death as learning the newspaper off by heart and reciting it to your husband. Impatient persons were advised, 'The white of an egg well beaten up with quicklime, and a small quantity of very old cheese, forms an excellent substitute for cement, when wanted in a hurry.' For instance, when you're walling someone up after dinner.

What sort of person required all this advice? He seems to have been a man who covered his boils with magnesium sulphate prior to scurrying up to the bedroom with a pail of water that would absorb the odour of fresh paint, before settling down to a long morning brushing his seaweed collection with gum mastic, pausing occasionally to fill a kettle with small marbles (keeps the fur away) or to examine the back of his throat for signs of anthrax.

There seemed never to be any loose ends. 'A girl of 18 earning a fair wage and having no one but herself to care for,' said the *Girls' Own Paper*, 'should be able to save 2s weekly, or £5.4s per annum. By the time she is 25 years old, her savings and the interest thereon would amount to £42. This sum, combined with the savings of her prospective husband, should prove amply sufficient to commence housekeeping on her own account.' Five pounds four shillings multiplied by seven. No undulation in the actual life of the paragon under review disturbs the arithmetic. 'You should not look in the faces of your superiors when passing them in the street, but if they first notice you, nod gravely.' The bits of advice sit like bricks in a walled-up window, stopping the light they are supposed to throw, eliminating the girl whose determination to save two shillings a week is spoiled by a weakness for beetle-drives, or the upstart who quite without encouragement shouts 'Hullo, cock' to Mr Gladstone.

But no one in the advice business seemed to doubt that to every exactly phrased question there was an equally exact answer. 'Two sisters may live very satisfactorily in the country on an income of one pound per week.' What the agony columns were selling in 1880 was the fairy gold of total certainty. 'Those who leave a warm room for a cold one, to dress for an evening party, must inevitably put their lives at risk. Thousands by so doing have received their death blow.' Which of the working girls who read the *Girls' Own Paper* would not happily have suffered those inevitable consequences, if the dress, not to mention the evening party – essential parts of the equation – had been as certain?

Something that kept creeping into the replies was the writer's chronic irritation that people who had no business to address him insisted on doing so. 'One, wear a frill round your neck, two, consult a doctor, three, your writing is unformed.' 'The enclosed poetry is harmless. We are sure it amused you to write it.' 'It is conceited to be nervous. Nobody wants to hear *you* play, it is the music of the composer they wish for.' 'You might as well cry for the moon in your position as a domestic servant. If eligible for a different calling, enabling you to have a home of your own, you *might* have a piano and practise if you liked.' Just now and again the answer supplied hinted that the down-trodden readership may have formulated a question that was not entirely serious. 'We know of no Institute to which old kid gloves are of value.' 'We cannot undertake to give a recipe for making woollen parrots.' 'The man who sent you a mouse in a matchbox could scarcely be called a gentleman.' But these were faint signs of rebellion. The keynote was constraint, people had to do what was expected of them, there were no blurred edges. The rigidness of the categories – hope, despair, happiness, melancholy, right, wrong, clever, dull – suggested life was a prison. At least the unctuous ingratiatory style the agony columnists now use to their readers makes it clear that today, at least, the prisoners have got money, and their gaolers must dance to their tune.

An Encounter with Solzhenitsyn

I met Alexander Solzhenitsyn when his book *Lenin in Zurich* came out. He was wearing a very thick hairy suit in black herring-bone (tweed, I think). I wondered if the furrow between his brows was a wound or a frown. He spoke continuously of his harsh life. I was agitated by the thought of having to speak to him about his book, since all his books have been written out of a suffering he has personally endured, and even though the book was not itself a suffering or a sentient thing – was in fact a novel and thus a work of the imagination

– nonetheless I was uneasy about treating it as I would have treated any other book.

I was also bothered by something else. Most writers are obsessed by things that have not happened to them, but what Solzhenitsyn is obsessed with actually took place. Does this fact make 'obsessed' the wrong word? To say Solzhenitsyn is obsessed with what happened to him is to make what happened sound small – when what happened to him *created* him. But supposing he is obsessed – is an obsessive – in the smaller way, as well? What if he is an awkward customer, into the bargain? I think I am saying this: the nobility of the man, the nobility of the art, places one in a position it is quite impossible to prepare for.

He kissed the hand of Miss Cyrilova from Cambridge who was to translate for us, and though I thought this must be very Russian I was slightly confused by my own inclination to do the same. When he laughed, it was as though laughter were a function of politeness, but never because he was amused. He went into the lavatory, and when he came out there was a bead of moisture on the heavy black cloth of his trouser-leg. I noticed this because, of our common humanity, it was the single, only thing I felt any right to claim a share of.

I asked him whether *Lenin in Zurich* was in fact a novel.

A.S.: I should say that it is a form of creative research. My aim is to reconstruct history in its fullness, in its authenticity, in its complexity: but for this I have to use the artist's vision, because a historian uses only documentary material, much of which has been lost. The historian uses evidence from witnesses, most of whom are no longer alive, and he tries to understand events, whereas the artist can see further, deeper, thanks to the force of perception in the artist's vision. I am not writing a novel. I am using all the artistic means available to penetrate as deeply as possible into historical events.

R.R.: Yes, but it must be a great difficulty to write history in the form of fiction where you have a real man and real events, and yet you have him as the centre of a fiction, and you have a scenario, which is also to some extent fictional, based on the real events.

A.S.: Just to describe invented characters would be impossible for me, and very boring. Imaginary characters are put in by authors, in most cases, where an author wants to establish a link between ordinary human psychology and historical events.

But it is impossible to portray historical events of the kind and magnitude we experienced, without a straightforward description of the historical figures who were involved. Only the writer, the artist, can achieve true insight into a historical character. There is a phenomenon called the 'tunnelling effect of intuition', which makes it possible for the artist to penetrate into regions closed to the historian-documentist, who can present only the factual evidence and the events surrounding it.

R.R.: You've said of this work, and also of the work which preceded it, *August 1914*, that 'it is the chief artistic design of my life'. Perhaps you'd explain that design.

A.S.: If one could explain such a design in a few simple words, there would be no need to write a long book. It is impossible to explain a work of art only on one level. But you are right: both *August 1914* and *Lenin in Zurich* are fragments of a long epic to which I am dedicating the rest of my life. I could not tackle it earlier owing to the difficult conditions I was living in, but I have been carrying it within me for forty years now, since 1936.

R.R.: There is a line from the writer James Joyce which puts me in mind of your own work. He spoke of 'trying to forge the uncreated conscience of my race' – a difficult line to translate for you, it's difficult even to paraphrase in the same language, but I'm wondering whether that chimes with you, whether in any sense you too are trying to forge the uncreated conscience of your race?

A.S.: Yes, you know, perhaps I am trying to do something which is very close to this. But there are certain differences resulting from our Russian conditions. There has been an absolutely deliberate attempt to break the 'weave of time', to use Shakespeare's expression. There has been a virtual erasing of the memory of what has happened, so for the consciousness of our national identity to re-emerge, I feel it is most important, first of all, to restore and correct the record of actual historical events. Only then will we be able to 'forge our uncreated conscience'. So, yes, this does come very close to our situation, your question is relevant.

R.R.: Let us come to Lenin, as depicted in your book. One of the things you say is that Lenin couldn't take a joke. Now I wonder whether that is your deduction, or whether that is something you actually know through the documentation?

A.S.: The forty years which I have spent working on this series of books, on this epic, I have also been working on Lenin. I have been consistently collecting every crumb of evidence about him, memoirs, reminiscences about his real character. I have not endowed him with any characteristic he did not possess. My aim is to give as little play to the imagination as possible and to recreate as closely as possible what he was really like.

The imagination of the writer only helps to forge the separate elements into one whole and, by penetrating into the character, to try to explain how these elements interact. This applies not only to his being unable to take a joke, but to various other traits of his character as well.

R.R.: I wonder why these revolutionaries, these politicians, tended to change their names – I'm thinking of Lenin and Parvus and Stalin and Trotsky – as though they were actors.

A.S.: It's a very interesting and, I should say, a very important question. In the beginning, as revolutionaries, they probably changed their names in order to escape from police surveillance, or as cover in correspondence to avoid mentioning their real names. But the interesting thing is this. After the revolution, when they came to power, they all kept their pseudonyms.

It is a most important question which you have asked. The author writing in some light literary genre, or a poet perhaps, has every right to change his name, or to adopt a pseudonym. He may be diffident or shy. But in people who are thinking of turning half the world, or the whole world, upside down, I consider there to be something dishonest in continuing to hide behind pseudonyms. They should proceed openly and call themselves by their real names. This diffidence seems to show a reluctance to accept any responsibility for their actions.

R.R.: Another interesting point to me was that Lenin talked much, in the story, of war and suffering, and the strife and pain that is inevitable if you're going to do what he's trying to do, make a revolution. But, at the same time, he evokes little of the paradise that is to ensue. I was wondering, as I read, whether those who used these cruel means ever abandoned them after they ceased to be necessary.

A.S.: I think that there is a devouring force in cruelty and violence which tends to take over those who make use of it. And even if, at the beginning, some people had idealistic aims for the future, they could not escape from this devouring force in real life. In fact, the first part of *The Gulag Archipelago* answers this question: what Lenin really did after coming to power. When all the powers of the intellect and of the spirit are geared towards the seizure of power, there is very little spiritual strength left for thinking about the promised paradise.

R.R.: At the time of which you write, Lenin was unknown, he was a nobody. How did this nobody magnetize so many?

A.S.: At the period I am dealing with, when Lenin was in Zurich, he really was a nobody. Historical events could easily have taken a course which would have left him a nobody. Two months before our Russian Revolution, he considered his life's work to have failed, and he was ready to go to America to finish his life in retirement there. However, even then he had a very strong personal influence on a small group of people around him.

When he moved into higher spheres of power, his influence spread over millions, but at this point it was not his personal charm or magnetism that was influential, since he no longer had such contact with individuals, and there was no television or radio. What took over here was the extraordinary power of his simplified slogans. They were so attractive, so magnetic, that they deceived the masses and led them along a false trail. They were promised everything, but were given nothing or had everything taken away.

R.R.: And then did his ultimate success depend to some extent on the fact that people were easily deceived?

A.S.: Yes, none of Lenin's main slogans were ever completely carried out – for example, workers' control of the means of production – or else they were falsely implemented for a number of years – for example, 'land of the peasants'. As early as 1922, ownership of the land was taken away from the peasants and transferred to the state.

His success lay in the fact that at the height of the war he promised an immediate end to the war and that no one would have to fight. This brought him millions of supporters from among the soldiers. But within only a year, the Soviet régime had introduced obligatory military service. And these same soldiers were conscripted for a three-year war. Those who refused were shot. This did not happen in Tsarist Russia: in Tsarist Russia, desertion carried a prison sentence.

But, under Lenin, desertion entailed immediate and even mass execution. So on all the main issues – war and peace, land, industry and factories, and what was supposed to be democratic rule – all these issues were promoted by deceitful slogans which were all broken in the very first years of Lenin's rule – under Lenin, I must emphasize, not under Stalin.

R.R.: I should like to ask you, Mr Solzhenitsyn, whether you feel you became a writer because of your experiences as an adult, or would you, do you feel, have become a writer whatever had happened to you?

A.S.: Somehow, the vague desire to become a writer arose in me very early, at the age of eight or nine. I had already begun to write before the war, in my youth, and I was hoping to have something published after the war. But then, later, my harsh experience of life – in prison and labour camps – simply changed the course of my work and, enriched by this experience, I had to give it expression. Nevertheless, although I had changed course, I was still heading in the same direction. And, as I said, I first thought of this epic in 1936, long before the war, when I had just finished my secondary schooling.

R.R.: Are there writers in the West, whether of the past or present, with whom you find an affinity?

A.S.: As a boy, I read a great many Western writers of the past, and together with Russian literature they formed my consciousness as a writer and influenced my writing methods. I am very much attached to Charles Dickens, for example. I read Dickens right through several times – but then the experience of my life became very violent, very harsh.

As you can see from my books, I spent a great deal of time on secret planning, which a writer should not have to waste his time on. I also had to work as a mathematician and teacher. Altogether, my basic work as a writer – so secret, so hidden – filled my life to such an extent that I simply had no time for ordinary life, no time just to read a book or to follow literary events. I had no time to live, not even eight hours for sleep.

Because of this, and as I do not know many languages, I have not been in constant touch with Western literature in recent years. So I would find it difficult to say who is spiritually closest to me as a writer, or whose creative methods I prefer.

R.R.: Your response to your experience has of course, been artistic. Could you ever envisage it as having been political? Could you see yourself as a politician of any sort?

A.S.: I am no politician, and I would not like to be a politician, but unfortunately the theme of my work, of my historical work, and, on the other hand, the cruel experience of my people, put me face to face with questions which inevitably have a political character. By tradition, Russian literature has been almost unable to isolate itself or to cut itself off from real events. Thus the bitter reality of our bitter experience makes it impossible for us to create artistically while paying no attention to social and political themes. But I myself am not a politician, and would not like to be one.

Lost November

I was in a stationer's shop where I was buying, on the strict understanding it was the poorest and cheapest, a ream of typing paper. In came a small mouselike lady bearing in her hand a small dog-eared pocket diary. She waved it in front of the white-haired whiskery beldam in a flowered overall who should by rights not have been running a stationer's shop but offering slightly too little for slightly too much in a tea-shop in Knutsford, and then spoke up in a timid thin South African voice: 'I'm sorry,' said Miss Mouse, waving the book about under the nose of the lady stationer, who now I think of it looked like Admiral Jellicoe, 'I'm sorry, but this diary you sold me has no November.' The Admiral, sensing mutiny, said, 'Well what's the good of bringing it back now when you bought it last January?' Miss Mouse said, smiling sadly, 'I'm sorry about that too, but when you buy a diary you don't read it through to make sure it's got November – you assume it's got the full twelve months, not eleven, and what can you do when you get to November and find it isn't there?' The First Sea Lord leant over the counter in her pinny and said sepulchrally, 'Happily, nothing whatever happens in November – at least,' she added, 'not in South-West One.' Miss Mouse burst into tears, and I made an excuse and left. I can't think which moved me more – the vulnerability of Miss Mouse (eleven-month diaries only happen to people like her) or the cheek of the Admiral.

The Mousetrap
– *Twenty-Sixth Year*

In the interval I got talking to two Irishmen and one of them said, 'I could tell you, I could indeed, I could tell you who done it, oh God I'm sorely tempted, shall I tell him, Mick, oh God I've a terrible desire to tell the man.' He explained his impulse was not malicious like those cab-drivers who delivered people to the theatre and, if the tip wasn't up to expectations, yelled the name of the murderer after them. He was simply impatient. He'd seen the play five years before, but his brother had tickets and he'd nothing better to do so he'd come again. 'Oh, God it's a boring play, have you ever in your life seen such a – have you? Shall I tell him, Mick? He'd leave, he'd leave, he'd walk out. I'll tell him, I will. Will I tell you? But then, oh God,' said the man, 'you're having a night out, so you are. Am I right, Michael? Yes, yes,' he said, 'all things considered you did well enough to come.' He waved his hand towards the stage. 'It's a natural object of pilgrimage.'

Later the manager of the theatre did a first-class impression of a group of Pakistanis ringing up the box-office as soon as the plane touched down and saying, 'We are all strict Mohammedans, we insist on seeing it.' Apparently they grow hysterical if the house is full. 'Fit us in, fit us in.' The manager waved his arms a bit too much, but it only needed polishing. He also reminisced about a patron in the circle-bar who had introduced him to his wife and then announced, 'When I saw this play for the first time, I was a Cub.' The manager had a vision of unborn generations queueing in the lady's womb.

I went back and sat down and couldn't fathom how it had lasted. Unless after a bit, after a year or two, a long run had produced a longer run by a process of hypnosis – people not being able to resist the permanence of the thing. And of course the theatre itself is very snug, really cosy, the sort of place you might expect to find small individual coal-fires let into the back of the seats. The curtain went up for the second half and the chocolates stirred excitedly in their wrappings.

'It's none of your damn business.'

'Can't you see she's all in?'

'Keep away from my wife, do you hear?'

'All cooked up between you, eh?'

'How blind you are.'

'You should have told me.'

'I wanted to forget.'

Armed to the teeth with blunt instruments of that sort, the cast forces life out, forces dialogue in. 'Oh Giles, do you think it will work out?' But I am wondering how often the hems of her skirt have been raised and lowered, how many different hairstyles she's had, as fashions changed in the distant world beyond the mullions and the Jacobean panels (the man who designed the set has given up the theatre long since, it was Roger Furse, who used to live next door to me, who retired to a Greek island to paint pictures, a natural staging-post on the way to the Elysian Fields, of which in the twenty-sixth year of *The Mousetrap* he has been an inhabitant for two decades). 'Schizo – schizowhatsit?' asks the sergeant, mispronouncing words to prove he's a member of that comic brotherhood, the lower classes. On one side of the fire (the hellish fire that everyone acts to – hand-rubbing, shivering, log-poking, etc.) there's a rack with magazines. When the play opened, it held such long-dead publications as *Everybody's Weekly*, *John O'Londons*, *Man About Town*. Chunner, chunner, chunner from the stage – a foggy consoling undramatic noise, oddly reminiscent of a public library at closing-time. The actors act from just behind their teeth, unloading the narrative like removal men whose simple business is to deliver.

Slowly I realize who dunnit and my feet go twitchy. I start trying to read the advertisements in the programme. 'You've guessed it, you've got it,' muttered the Irishman seated beside me. 'Michael, he knows, he knows, I think he knows, I see the symptoms. Who do you think it was, who was it now, who was it, let's see if you know –' 'Shhh' hissed a lady in the row behind. The Irishman turned round and fixed the lady with his eye and whispered accusingly, 'It was *you*, so it was.'

Nevill Coghill

I had two strange feelings about him, even before I met him – that he was some ideal long-lost relative I was about to be reunited with, and at the same time that he was a mythological figure and any notion of actually making his acquaintance was about as absurd as thinking you might run into Dr Johnson or Sir Patrick Spens.

Jack the porter pointed across the quad and said, 'If Mr Coghill's your tutor, that's him.' And I saw the tall gaunt figure, and this larger-than-life feeling I'd had about him ever since hearing the Somerville and Ross stories as well as the *Canterbury Tales* he'd been doing on the Home Service was suddenly augmented, and I thought, 'Crikey, he *is* Chaucer.'

But at the same time there was something fearfully unheroic about the man's hair – a sort of grey, wind-torn upland – not to mention the tweed trousers rising steadily towards half-mast (a good six inches of four-ply sock was visible above shoes that at some stage in their lives may well have been suede) that revived the other feeling that I was an orphan who was at last going to be taken care of.

We shook hands and I saw he had a great big face and a giant smile and he said he'd just come back from Castletownshend where he'd been out hunting with a man from England who had been so impressed with the way they did it in West Cork that he'd said, 'Compared to this, hunting in Leicestershire is like chasing a mouse round a pisspot.' And the giant smile broke open and let out a laugh like a corncrake and I, whose sporting reminiscences didn't encompass much more than the putting-green in the recreation ground, felt some small door in the wide world being opened, specially for me.

I stammered something about listening to him on the wireless with my mother and how much we'd enjoyed it, and he said, 'Mother liked it, did she?' I don't know how to explain it, but his use of that phrase made me feel terribly welcome.

I think of autumn when I think of his rooms, but in the summer we'd have tutorials outside, and once he read aloud to us *The Phoenix and the Turtle,* and at the end of the poem a tear stole down his cheek. In the same garden he picked a bunch of flowers for the girl I was with, and Dawkins (who'd known Swinburne, and lent money to Rolfe, and kept fourteen Greek dialects alive single-handed by speaking them himself) tottered over, thinking they were for him – 'Not these, professor dear,' he said, and picked him another bunch. Tenderness was his style, his watchword. His own tutor had been Onions, co-editor of the O.E.D., and when the great work was complete he went shyly up to Onions in the street to congratulate him, and Onions wailed, 'Oh, oh – I know it's a bad book – *don't* rub it in!' When he told the tale, his laughter was protective, it was Onions's vulnerability, his diffidence, that moved him.

How callow one was, breezing in and out, sure of his unlimited attention, as though one were a charge on him for life. I blush to think of it, and yet – selfish to the end – I think of his death and I feel abandoned. When I left Oxford, I hoped the world might be full of such men. But it wasn't.

The Fête

Every Saturday afternoon, all through the summer, the Member had to go and open a fête.

'I don't know whether you've ever seen one of those chromium-plated cake-stands, have you? Only at Zeeta's – quite. Well, we won one. Not exactly the sort of thing you can give anyone as a present, so we thought we'd donate it to the next fête. And do you know –' the Member studied me keenly, wondering if I was going to grasp that what he had to tell me next lay at the heart of the matter – 'We won the bloody thing again.'

We drove on through north Oxfordshire. Some spring of melancholy had been broached, and the Member said, 'I remember them all in terms of fuchsias. Loads and loads of fuchsias in pots, blowing over in the wind. You always have to buy one. Sometimes,' he said, 'they give you a great big carnation with five feet of fern adhering. They jam it into your buttonhole, and the fern tickles your chin all day.' He paused, dwelling on what he'd said. 'Fuchsias first, then women behind tea-urns, festooned in steam.'

We made for Charlbury. The fête was being held at the Marquis's place. He wouldn't be there, but he let them use his grounds.

'I once tied with the Marquis's butler, you know – bowling for the pig. Bowled and bowled, and finally got it. We fattened the pig, and then –' a spark which had kindled at the memory of the contest flickered and died '– we gave the proceeds to Party funds.' He glanced briefly at me again, as though we'd run up against another of the basic principles and he didn't want me to miss it. 'If you win anything good, you've got to give it back.'

Then he said, 'Jam. Jars and jars of jam. We're not a jam-eating family, as it happens, but you have to buy it. You have to buy everything,' he said, 'but my wife and I have a special sort of basket, sort of long boat-shaped affair, and our tactic is to stuff two big cauliflowers either end and a jar of this jam in the middle, and really it looks as if you've swept through the place like a locust and bought the lot.'

There was a spatter of rain across the windscreen, but the sun shone through it. 'I do a five-minute opener, and about half-way through a child disconnects the amplifier, or a Voodoo jet with re-heat on comes over just as I get to the punch line. The vicar kindly leads the laughter. I keep the politics general because nobody is listening – it's a bit like a cabaret, only instead of the clash of knives and forks you get the eager hum of females settling on the jumble.'

We bumped across the Marquis's pasture. His nice house had shutters over the windows, and the swimming-pool was roped off, but his shaven lawns were being walked on by people who seemed delighted just to be doing that.

'Even get Labour people – can't resist a peep behind the lodge gates. Half the fun of it, really. Don't walled gardens make you curious? Here we are. You'll see me smiling at people rather a lot,' said the Member, getting out of the car. 'Hullo, ha, ha, ha,' he said, good as his word.

Music was winding out of the loudspeakers with that peculiar outdoor effect of being heavier than air. The Member walked across the sward, shaking hands with ladies from the village who kept laughing among themselves as though the business of encountering each other in public were somehow inexpressibly saucy. Someone wrenched the needle off the record, and it made a noise through the tannoy like a pair of trousers tearing. The Member walked on to the terrace in front of the long windows, and stood behind a trestle-table that was draped in a voluminous Union Jack.

Said he was glad to be there. Hoped they were too. Felt sure that occasions like these were good for morale. Thought all Conservatives had a duty to go out into the highways and byways and spread the gospel. Urged everyone to lose no opportunity of 'widening the family in the good old Conservative way'. Had pleasure in declaring the fête open. Applause.

A small band beneath a mournful cypress struck up, and the rain rustled in the Marquis's elms. All the pennies at the roll'em stall clattered to the back when rolled because the stall was on a slope. 'Conditions are not ideal,' shouted a man through a megaphone, 'for weight-lifting, but Fred is going to attempt a snatch of a hundred and forty pounds.'

The Member approached the hoop-la stall. 'Sometimes you can't get away from the rostrum after the opening because an earnest, deaf, elderly constituent who has strong feelings on Afghanistan presses you up against the microphone and keeps his face very close to yours.' The hoop-la combined frivolity with perfect utility – prizes included a tin of Smedley's Golden Swede Turnips, a packet of Ty-phoo, and a bicycle-lamp. The Member won some Elizabeth Lazenby Portuguese Sardines. 'Actually, they were the only sort we were allowed as children.'

In a light rain, the folk-dancers waited patiently with their heads raised, while the tannoy ground through two wrong tunes and started on a third. 'I'm very sorry, ladies and gentlemen, but I keep getting it on to an inappropriate section of the record,' the announcer said. But one of the dancers ran off and fixed it for him, and then they did a dance, dressed in orange skirts and velvet waistcoats, while a small child took a picture of them, using a Box Brownie left over from the days when radio was called the wireless.

The Member ate a large dog-eared egg-sandwich the size of a pocket handkerchief, and tucked under his arm a bottle of Super-Active Nimbus, a pair of socks, and a coat-hanger covered in yellow knitting. The grass had a sweet, mashed smell, and it blended with heavier, more languorous exhalations rolling across the pasture from the hedges of box. The band, with unaggressive devotion, played 'Ye

Banks and Braes of Bonny Doon', and the sound that came out of their silver instruments was pleasant for its very diffidence. Everyone smiled, pleased with their own presence, and pleased with the presence of everyone else.

I bought the Member a jam-sponge, and left with the sort of regret I could never have predicted.

The Last Interview with Nabokov

We arrived in February. Wintry laurels and the bare willow trees made the path at the side of the lake seem melancholy, and there was a curious feeling of taking a walk in an old photograph. We were calling on Nabokov to let him know we were there, and also to tell him he'd given us rather short measure. The Nabokov interview is an entirely structured affair: the questions are sent a fortnight or so before the event, the answers are composed and returned, and then all you have to do is get in front of a camera and *serve* the interview, like iced cake. But it was to be a 25-minute programme, and he hadn't given us quite enough.

He had been very ill. When he came into one of the public rooms of that slightly left-over caravanserai, the Montreux-Palace Hotel, he was leaning on a stick, his face was pale, and his collar was now a size or two too large for the neck. Mme Nabokov was with him, and because she too had been ill she had a bent and hooded look. I felt rather scared, I don't quite know why, and to my surprise, after we'd been talking for a few minutes and I'd said how agreeable it was to know the interview had already taken place, frozen on paper before the cameras arrived, precluding the possibility of anything unexpected, Mme Nabokov murmured in a low voice, 'Were you frightened?' I jumped and cried, 'Oh no, not at all, not a bit,' but I suppose in accepting the premise of so strange a question, I gave myself the lie.

As far as the length of the interview was concerned, it was plain that Nabokov had said all that he wished to say and wished to say no more.

So it was decided that he would read one of his poems, and immediately, like a chef measuring out his ingredients in extraordinarily careful spoonfuls, he began to weigh the poem in terms of time – 'So many *strophes* at so many seconds a *strophe*, let us say fifteen *strophes* –' 'No, it is twelve,' interjected Mme Nabokov – 'twelve, then say thirty seconds for each *strophe*, multiplied by twelve, that gives us an extra six minutes, yes, it is quite enough –'

We weren't allowed into the Nabokov quarters – six rooms on the top floor of the Hotel ('those *attics*', as Nabokov drily apostrophized them). We were excluded on the grounds of there not being space enough, but it would have been odd if a man who had devoted his life to holding the world entertainingly at bay should not have protected his privacy. So a faint social hiccup developed – we were calling on business, but they actually *lived* at the Hotel, so that when Nabokov said, 'We could go into the bar, if you wished to offer a drink,' I thought he must have meant 'If you wish to *be* offered a drink'; but not only was this a slightly absurd indulgence to extend to a writer who always takes pains to say precisely what he wants to say, it just didn't quite feel as though the Nabokovs were 'At Home' . . .

We drank some vodka ('Crepkaya, if it is for M. Nabokov', the waiter murmured) and Nabokov explained that he would like some vodka on the table in front of him when the interview was filmed the following day – 'but because I do not wish to give a false impression and have people think I am an old drunk, let them put the vodka in a water-jug'. In short, he was saying that the illness had laid him low, and the camera and the bright lights would tax his strength. When we got up to go, he said, 'Who is the potentate?' and I realized – again with a faint twinge of embarrassment – he was saying, 'You pay.'

The next day a room at the Montreux-Palace was lit for the cameras, and Nabokov seated himself at one of those Louis-the-Hotel tables and propped his notes against the carafe which held the vodka, and we did the question-and-answer as I imagine Elizabethan actors conducted a duologue – moving stiffly through a sequence of conventional gestures and inflections which had been devised to relieve the participants of the idiocy of pretending the exchange was spontaneous. Neither Nabokov nor I made any attempt at *mime*, we lifted the cards to our eyes and read the words we had already exchanged on paper, aloud: at the end of the dance, I as it were handed my partner back to his seat, and put on my glasses to read the words, 'Thank you, Mr Nabokov.'

When the film ran out, by times, we conversed. Nabokov said, 'I once had an interview with a man who suspected that my feelings for Lolita were something other than a father might feel towards his child.' His tone, his manner, as he spoke, seemed coquettish. Was he coaxing me into the banality of an inquiry? I said, referring to the journalist he was talking about, 'That was a bit crass of him.' But Nabokov looked a little sulky, a little disappointed. 'Oh no,' he said, 'not crass, not necessarily.' I said spinsterishly, 'I don't think it's a question I'd want to ask you.' Nabokov said, 'Oh, I think *I* would. I think *I* would.' And smiled, but not engagingly.

After a while, Nabokov said, 'Do you think Lewis Carroll actually did anything with those little girls he photographed?' I found the question alarmingly anecdotal, from a member of the Pantheon. I said, giving the matter a second or two's thought, 'I doubt it. If he had, he wouldn't have needed to write the books or take the pictures, would he?' Again I felt I had given the wrong answer. Nabokov shook his head. 'No, no, no. There was something going on.' I said, 'But I could imagine the works, the stories, the fantasies, were *instead* of all that?' Nabokov smiled a smile that was full of bad news. He said, 'There was a lay in it somewhere. There was a *lay* in it somewhere.' Throughout the interview, throughout the asides, Mme Nabokov had sat in a corner of the room, her hands clasped on her walking-stick, quite silent. I sensed her presence behind me throughout, and as I faced Nabokov, I felt her absorption too, he was all her care. The Nabokovs moved slowly out of the room, and I had some idea they were returning to a chess game they had left unfinished upstairs.

R.R.: First, sir, to spare you irritation, I wonder if you will instruct me in the pronunciation of your name.

V.N.: Let me put it this way. There exists a number of deceptively simple-looking Russian names, whose spelling and pronunciation present the foreigner with strange traps. The name Suvarov took a couple of centuries to lose the preposterous middle 'a' – it should be Suvoruv. American autograph-seekers, while professing a knowledge of all my books – prudently not mentioning their titles – rejuggle the vowels of my name in all the ways allowed by mathematics. 'Nabakav' is especially touching for the 'a's. Pronunciation problems fall into a less erratic pattern. On the playing-fields of Cambridge, my football team used to hail me as 'Nabkov' or, facetiously, 'Macnab'. New Yorkers reveal their tendency of turning 'o' into 'ah' by pronouncing my name 'Nabarkov'. The aberration '*Nabokov*' is a favourite one of postal officials. Now, the correct Russian way would take too much time to explain, and so I've settled for euphonious 'Na*bo*kov', with the middle syllable accented and rhyming with 'smoke'. Would you like to try?

R.R.: Mr Na*bo*kov.

V.N.: That's right.

R.R.: You grant interviews on the understanding that they shall not be spontaneous. This admirable method ensures there will be no dull patches. Can you tell me why and when you decided upon it?

V.N.: I'm not a dull speaker, I'm a bad speaker, I'm a wretched speaker. The tape of my unprepared speech differs from my written prose as much as the worm differs from the perfect insect – or, as I once put it, I think like a genius, I write like a distinguished author and I speak like a child.

R.R.: You've been a writer all your life. Can you evoke for us the earliest stirring of the impulse?

V.N.: I was a boy of fifteen, the lilacs were in full bloom. I had read Pushkin and Keats. I was madly in love with a girl of my age, I had a new bicycle (an Enfield, I remember) with reversible handlebars that could turn it into a racer. My first poems were awful, but then I reversed those handlebars, and things improved. It took me, how-ever, ten more years to realize that my true instrument was prose – poetic prose, in the special sense that it depended on comparisons and metaphors to say what it wanted to say. I spent the years 1925 to 1940 in Berlin, Paris and the Riviera, after which I took off for America. I cannot complain of neglect on the part of any great critics, although as always and everywhere there was an odd rascal or two badgering me. What has amused me in recent years is that those old novels and stories published in English in the sixties and seventies were appreci-ated much more warmly than they had been in Russian thirty years ago.

R.R.: Has your satisfaction in the act of writing ever fluctuated? I mean, is it keener now or less keen than once it was?

V.N.: Keener.

R.R.: Why?

V.N.: Because the ice of experience now mingles with the fire of inspiration.

R.R.: Apart from the pleasure it brings, what do you conceive your task as a writer to be?

V.N.: This writer's task is the purely subjective one of reproducing as closely as possible the image of the book he has in his mind. The reader need not know, or, indeed, cannot know, what the image is, and so cannot tell how closely the book has conformed to its image in the author's mind. In other words, the reader has no business bothering about the author's intentions, nor has the author any business trying to learn whether the consumer likes what he consumes.

R.R.: Of course, the author works harder than the reader does. But I wonder whether it augments his – this is to say, your – pleasure that he makes the reader work hard, too.

V.N.: The author is perfectly indifferent to the capacity and condition of the reader's brain.

R.R.: Could you give us some idea of the pattern of your working day?

V.N.: This pattern has lately become blurry and inconstant. At the peak of the book, I work all day, cursing the tricks that objects play upon me, the mislaid spectacles, the spilled wine. I also find talking of my working day far less entertaining than I formerly did.

R.R.: The conventional view of an hotel is as of a temporary shelter – one arrives as a traveller, after all – yet you choose to make it permanent.

V.N.: I have toyed on and off with the idea of buying a villa. I can imagine the comfortable furniture, the efficient burglar alarms, but I am unable to visualize an adequate staff. Old retainers require time to get old, and I wonder how much of it there still is at my disposal.

R.R.: You once entertained the possibility of returning to the United States. I wonder if you will.

V.N.: I will certainly return to the United States at the first opportunity. I'm indolent, I'm sluggish, but I'm sure I'll go back with tenderness. The thrill with which I think of certain trails in the Rockies is only matched by visions of my Russian woods, which I will never revisit.

R.R.: Is Switzerland a place with positive advantages for you, or is it simply a place without positive disadvantages?

V.N.: The winters can be pretty dismal here, and my old borzoi has developed feuds with lots of local dogs, but otherwise it's all right.

R.R.: You think and write in three languages – which would be the preferred one?

V.N.: Yes, I write in three languages, but I think in images. The matter of preference does not really arise. Images are mute, yet presently the silent cinema begins to talk and I recognize its language. During the second part of my life, it was generally English, my own brand of English – not the Cambridge variety, but still English.

R.R.: At any point do you invite your wife to comment on work in progress?

V.N.: When the book is quite finished, and its fair copy is still warm and wet, my wife goes carefully through it. Her comments are usually few but invariably to the point.

R.R.: Do you find that you re-read your own earlier work, and if you do, with what feelings?

V.N.: Re-reading my own works is a purely utilitarian business. I have to do it when correcting a paperback edition riddled with misprints or controlling a translation, but there are some rewards. In certain species – this is going to be a metaphor – in certain species, the wings of the pupated butterfly begin to show in exquisite miniature through the wing-cases of the chrysalis a few days before emergence. It is the pathetic sight of an iridescent future transpiring through the shell of the past, something of the kind I experience when dipping into my books written in the twenties. Suddenly through a drab photograph a blush of colour, an outline of form, seems to be distinguishable. I'm saying this with absolute scientific modesty, not with the smugness of ageing art.

R.R.: Which writers are you currently reading with pleasure?

V.N.: I'm re-reading Rimbaud, his marvellous verse and his pathetic correspondence in the Pléiade edition. I am also dipping into a collection of unbelievably stupid Soviet jokes.

R.R.: Your praise for Joyce and Wells has been high. Could you identify briefly the quality in each which sets them apart?

V.N.: Joyce's *Ulysses* is set apart from all modern literature, not only by the force of his genius, but also by the novelty of his form. Wells is a great writer, but there are many writers as great as he.

R.R.: Your distaste for the theories of Freud has sometimes sounded to me like the agony of one betrayed, as though the old magus had once fooled you with his famous three-card trick. Were you ever a fan?

V.N.: What a bizarre notion! Actually I always loathed the Viennese quack. I used to stalk him down dark alleys of thought, and now we shall never forget the sight of old, flustered Freud seeking to unlock his door with the point of his umbrella.

R.R.: The world knows that you are also a lepidopterist but may not know what that involves. In the collection of butterflies, could you describe the process from pursuit to display?

V.N.: Only common butterflies, showy moths from the tropics, are put on display in a dusty case between a primitive mask and a vulgar abstract picture. The rare, precious stuff is kept in the glazed drawers of museum cabinets. As for pursuit, it is, of course, ecstasy to follow an undescribed beauty skimming over the rocks of its habitat, but it is also great fun to locate a new species among the broken insects in an old biscuit tin sent over by a sailor from some remote island.

R.R.: One can always induce a mild vertigo by recalling that Joyce might not have existed as the writer but as the tenor. Have you any sense of having narrowly missed some other role? What substitute could you endure?

V.N.: Oh, yes, I have always had a number of parts lined up in case the muse failed. A lepidopterist exploring famous jungles came first, then there was the chess grandmaster, then the tennis ace with an unreturnable service, then the goalie saving a historic shot, and finally, finally, the author of a pile of unknown writings – *Pale Fire*, *Lolita*, *Ada* – which my heirs discover and publish.

R.R.: Alberto Moravia told me of his conviction that each writer writes only of one thing – has but a single obsession he continually develops. Can you agree?

V.N.: I have not read Alberto Moravia, but the pronouncement you quote is certainly wrong in my case. The circus tiger is not obsessed by his torturer, my characters cringe as I come near with my whip. I have seen a whole avenue of imagined trees losing their leaves at the threat of my passage. If I do have any obsessions, I'm careful not to reveal them in fictional form.

R.R.: Mr Nabokov, thank you.

V.N.: You're welcome, as we say in my adopted country.

Good Morning

I walked into the dentist's waiting-room and saw there was only one other chap there, so – question – do I say good morning? Easier to say than not to say, because once the acknowledgement's made you can both forget about each other. So O K – 'Good morning.' There was a sort of rumbling noise from the other chap, as of a drawbridge rusty with disuse being reluctantly let down, and he said, 'Good morning,' only he stretched the words out resentfully, as though they were someone's collected works I'd forced him to read, as though I'd really given him an awful lot of trouble, as though I'd presumed on the fact of us both being in the same room to invite him to a Tupperware party.

So I thought right, that'll teach me. And the next week I had to go again, but this time I was the first in the waiting-room, and another chap came in, about eight feet tall and wearing an anorak that curiously seemed to come down to his ankles, and I thought, Right, mate, *you* can say good morning to *me*. But he didn't. He scrabbled about among the mags on the table, and then did the unforgivable thing. There were lots of comfortable chairs and perches in the room and I'd sat modestly on a small settle at one end, and lo, instead of choosing one of the other seats, this geezer picked up his copy of *Horse and Hound* and without saying a word sat plump next to me on the same sofa, crowding me over to one side. One thing to give the time of day – it sets the limit of the relationship – but to sit next to a chap when you might have sat anywhere else is either to pretend he isn't there at all, or to assume an intimacy that doesn't exist. I was thinking of wrong-footing him by asking whether the vet only doctored cats on a Friday or – and then I was going to fumble in my pocket – whether it was all right to bring in a stoat, when the nurse called him out, possibly to have his anorak removed under anaesthetic.

I don't like standoffishness, but on the other hand there are women of sixty-five touring the West Country cathedrals, travelling always in pairs and driving Triumph Sodomite motorcars, who insist on saying good morning to everyone at breakfast-time in hotels – one total stranger in a twin-set once asked me how I'd slept. Good morning is often a preliminary to a life-story, and I sometimes think that what makes the idea of a cruise so hideous is that it is good morning elevated into a way of life.

The Middle-aged Philistine Abroad

The second morning at the ski resort, I woke up and looked out of the window and was shaken by a spasm of rage.

'See what I see?' I asked my wife.

'What?'

'The snow.'

'Well?'

I turned to the window and shook my fist. 'You should ski down it once, and it should all go away.'

I caught the sound of my own voice, and found I objected to it. What I'd said was no more than the revealed truth about holidays: what everyone can't stand about holidays is the way you do the same thing every day, without anything happening. But there was a kind of edge on the way I spoke that made me sound like someone whose company I wouldn't want to keep.

Then we went to Moscow for the weekend (makes a change from the Cotswolds) and when we got back I started telling people it had been like spending four days at a post office with all the positions closed. And for the second time I caught an echo of myself, and I sounded like a man who'd been to Paris and couldn't get a cup of tea.

No one's going to deny I'm absolutely right about the food in America, nobody's going to argue about it being absolutely tasteless, but when I went round announcing that the national dish of America was menus, I think I heard myself saying it like journalists do when they're trying to pass off some personal inconvenience as a symptom of someone else's economic malaise.

In many ways I qualified for the VC in sending back a steak in a reputable but unsympathetic two-star Michelin restaurant one quiet day in Clichy, when all I had between myself and my naked desire not to eat what I couldn't swallow was the fraying selvedge of my grammar-school French. Yet though I got full marks from my chum (who hadn't helped the cause by eating all his, plus the plate as well), I couldn't like myself very much as we walked away – I'd been right, but somehow that wasn't enough.

Seeing myself as I appear in these small histories is like suddenly having the view blotted out by a fat woman in a cinema. As time wears on and I travel further, there's one bloody old fool I'd like to leave behind, one fearsome old bore whose luggage slows me down, one fatuous tourist who won't let somewhere else be somewhere else, one damned old idiot who thinks Abroad has to prove itself, one ageing noodle who constantly gets in his own way, and of course I'm talking about me.

I seem to have crept up on myself so that now when I travel my own presence is a sort of static, distracting me from the Pyramids, the Taj Mahal, the Salt Lake Desert. I'm like a pirate station I can't tune out, a ludicrous mutter which keeps on asking 'Did you really want to come? When do you start enjoying yourself? Is it time to go home yet?' I hang around my own holidays like Marley's ghost, looking for someone to accuse.

When I was nineteen, I felt Abroad was some joyous conspiracy I'd been let into, a place that excited me because it had always been there while I hadn't. Now Abroad is the American I sat next to on the way to Washington who in a bagpipe monotone briefed me in the art of folding a jacket so that it should not crease, repeating his instructions not once but twice, even contriving by some sleight of hand to get me to say it all back to him. To prove to his wife that he had absolute power over me, he actually forced me to my feet between the seats so that all three of us could celebrate the holiday he had just enjoyed by drinking a toast to my lovely Queen. One way or another I always get this man because, poor bugger, he always gets me. In a dreadful sort of way, we need each other.

On the rare occasions I'm prepared to be surprised, I think I have the decency to feel remorse for the middle-aged philistinism through which the surprise has to crash. As for example, one hot morning in Malaga we walked into what looked like the coolest and oldest of hotels. Punkahs rustled in the brown gloom and an aged waiter bowed as we gave our order. The room was full of seigneurial males, one of whom rose slowly to his feet and approached us. In a tone which combined gentleness with an entire absence of reproof he said, 'You have made an understandable mistake. This is a gentleman's club. You are now my guests.'

Or the *garagiste* mending a motorbike in a lane full of bees and thyme, not far from La Devinière. I asked the way, wondering if he could tell me if there was wine to be bought in these parts. Pausing with the inner tube in his hands, he said he personally had no wine for sale, but would like to show me his collection. He took me into his *cave* – literally that, a vast antre within a rocky scarp – and standing there in his bicycle-clips pointed to rack after rack, fifteen years of growths from the Loire. We sampled the Chinon and the Ligré, the Montlouis and the Bourgeuil, through a long afternoon. He looked upon the wines of Bordeaux as illegitimate, scarcely potable on the grounds of their alcohol. He brought forth a curiosity, one of a dozen bottles so powerfully corked that in fact it tasted like the most exquisite vermouth. He laughed as he drank a little of it. He was amused. All this was his hobby. He was an *amateur*.

I do not deserve such treats, and as those very words go down on the paper, slap, slap, from the typewriter, the telephone rings and I am offered my true deserts. A man invites me to go to Marbella and there for a consideration chair a seminar of what in his own words he calls 'the older and wiser heads in Hardware'. Marbella is to echo to the voices of men who make self-adhesive tiles, and I shall be free to suck at the same dug as the sons of Polyfilla. The open-handed man on the other end of the phone urges the weight of the occasion by candidly admitting his first choice had been Frank Bough – 'to give you some idea of the level at which you would be operating'.

I honestly felt some wag had been looking over my shoulder and had been laying for me with a moral in the shape of a blunt instrument. After all, if I don't like my own company as a traveller because I tend to exclude what I should include, where better to complete the sealing-off process than that concrete grove, Marbella, and what better to grout in the edges than a high-class product like Polycel? I might almost have gone, if I hadn't had to travel with myself.

Augustus Carp

I think I was twelve when my father brought the book in from a second-hand barrow in Farringdon Road, and from that time on for the next twenty or thirty years the thing became part of our family patois. We would muse sorrowfully over those 'heads of families who prefer the flicker of the cinematograph to the Athanasian Creed', urge friends to join with us in founding a new branch of 'The Anti-Dramatic and Saltatory Union', and earnestly debate the morality of descending from a bus while it was still in motion (one of the book's great themes).

We became so familiar with the characters in the story that we began to feel they were blood relatives: Alexander Carkeek, the prosperous fishmonger ('a northern Caledonian of the most offensive type') and his two sons, Cosmo and Corkran: the Rev. Eugene Cake, author of the fundamentalist novel *Gnashers of Teeth* ('It is even more powerful than *Without Are Dogs*'): Abraham Stool, proprietor of Stool's Adult Gripe Water (later removed to an asylum, 'Mr Stool was already under the impression that he was the Hebrew patriarch, and several times insisted upon my approaching him and placing my hand under his left thigh, after which he would offer me, in addition to Mrs Stool, a varying number of rams and goats . . .').

One day in the sixties, I was talking to Anthony Burgess and in the course of conversation improved my end of it with a graft from the great work (it might easily have been a pinch from the sermon delivered in praise of the new lectern by the Vicar of St James-the-Least-of-All – 'Yes, they were trustees. They must never forget that. That was a distinction he would have them remember. They were not only human beings, but they were churchmen and trustees – church beings, trustees and human men – yea, and women also [he trowed], churchees and trustmen – furniture women, church-trusts and humanees.').

'I don't believe it,' cried Burgess, 'I'm the only one who's ever read it!'

As for me, I felt Burgess was claiming common kinship, as though he'd jumped out of the same womb. He gave a password – he either said I was 'now in the full flower of my southern metropolitan Xtian manhood' (quite properly emphasizing the X), or possibly invited me to join him in 'an humorous glee'. And I knew I had met the first man beside myself who had ever heard of *Augustus Carp Esq: By himself: Being the Autobiography of a Really Good Man.*

The only other work it compares with is *Diary of a Nobody*, but where Pooter grovels, Carp is a swine. It's the tale of a lower-middle-class humbug, exaggerated to a point where it becomes a sort of ballad or poem. Brought up at Mon Repos, Angela Gardens, Camberwell ('one of some thirty-six admirably conceived houses of a similar and richly ornamented architecture'), and modelling himself on a father who combines low-Church vengefulness with total self-approval (and, moreover, 'in whose ears there resided the rare faculty of independent motion'), Carp divides his childhood between indigestion brought on by greed and an arcane attachment to the game of Nuts in May ('though I was short, with singularly slender arms, my abdomen was large and well covered, while my feet, with their exceptional length and breadth and almost imperceptible arches, enabled me to obtain a tenacious hold of the ground upon which they were set'), grows up to rebuke smokers on the upper decks of omnibuses, and suffers a dreadful fate ('port-poisoning') at the hands of an actress whose soul he is saving.

A comic creation of Stigginsian stature – but by whom? When the book came out in 1924, it was anonymous. Prompted by our meeting, Burgess egged Heinemann on to bring out a new edition, and in the course of doing so discovered who the genius was – no less a personage than the sometime Hon. Physician to King George VI! Alas, he died before the book was re-issued, but to my pleasure as I re-read *Augustus Carp* for the umpteenth time is added the essential mystery – out of what strange corner of himself was Sir Henry Howarth Bashford, Kt, MD, FRCP, delivered of a comic masterpiece?

Thoughts Provoked by a Distant Prospect of the Great Gear Trading Company

I quite often take strolls up and down the King's Road, it's the High Street of the district I live in, and I like a trot round the houses better than a real walk in the country. I like to go out for a thirteen-amp plug or a copy of *Private Eye*, and have a stare at what people are doing. It's not so much fun as it used to be, because most of the people in the King's Road aren't doing anything, they're just staring too – people from as far north as Finchley, or even Cockfosters, charter buses to come and do their staring in the King's Road, and ordinary neighbourhood staring – the sort of thing you do when you're doing something else as well – has got swamped in this more generalized version: it's as though staring has been removed from the individual and become something you probably have to join a club to do – Lords for cricket, Brighton for ping-pong, King's Road for staring. And people looking at people looking at people is pretty bland, ranking for blandness rather below ten-pin bowling and fractionally above keeping tropical fish.

But I still turn out and thread my way among the young, who are clad so variously that variety itself has become a uniform. I usually start my healthful ramble from round about the paper-shop at the end of Bramerton Street, and forge onwards to Sloane Square, my own my Peter Jones square, and even back again should the weather prove clement.

Which, on the day I have in mind, it didn't. It came on to rain round about Soldier Blue, and was pelting down as I got to Second Image. So quick as you like, I dodged into the Great Gear Trading Company, grabbing by their various arms both my wife and my mother who were out seeing the sights with me and doing a bit of shopping. Now this was something new, because theretofore I'd only enjoyed what you might call a distant prospect of the Great Gear Trading Company, and indeed of all such shops, like Second Image aforementioned, and Slot Machine and R. Soles and Downtown Saddles and Made in Heaven and Sugarcane and When Did You Last See Your Father, though I can't be sure that isn't a picture. I hadn't got close to these shops because I had the feeling they were holding me at bay. They have an unforgiving air of carnival, they *enjoin* the party spirit, and I find that awfully daunting, especially in a shop. The bright acid paint of the fronts, and the fat plastic letters of the names, parody the cumbersome commercial jollity of early comic books – a parody of the disposable, of something that's picked up and thrown away. But the metaphor leaks into the reality, for the shops themselves seem to fold up fairly regularly, and like the *Hotspur* and the *Wizard* and the *Adventure* of an earlier day, it doesn't really matter because there'll be another out next week.

There's usually a flatus of electronic sound, a lees of muzak – as it were the stalks and skin, left behind from the original jazz, after the third or fourth pressing – there's always this thin noise seeping out of shops like the Great Gear, and it hangs over the King's Road, turning into a fixed smile, a frozen smile, which invites the young to express themselves by spending. When I think of it, the verb 'spend' has brothelly Elizabethan overtones that I hadn't allowed for – apt enough because in spending *thus*, the young lose their power, and lose it to those who thereby accumulate it. If they want a new name to go over one of those shops – something to fit in with Fruit Fly and the Jean Machine and Flip – why not try A Bawd, Pompey, A Bawd?

I suppose about three quarters of all the shops in the King's Road now fit into this category. No sooner does the lease of a fishmonger's or a greengrocer's fall in than two clever actors open a restaurant or an antique shop (where do all the antiques *come* from? Same place as the Beaujolais, I suppose), or a man with an Afro hairstyle and an elementary but enthusiastic grasp of a balance-sheet decides he's had enough of being a punter and, instead of buying the clothes, opens a shop and starts selling them. Of course, you have to be blindly sentimental in the way the middle-aged find themselves being to feel that the shops these new shops replace were in any way superior. The old places were often staffed by bullet-headed curmudgeonly ancients who took it as a personal affront when anyone actually had the nerve to come in and buy anything. They were the sort of places – not all of them, but almost all of them some of the time – where the peculiarly relishing overtones that negatives acquired during the war were still preserved: 'Sorry – all gone' would still come out like someone mechanically responding in pidgin English to the natives. And of course the primitive Stone Age Old Testament retailer's spell against anything he chose to regard as exotic, namely 'We've no call for it – you're the third person today who's asked,' has passed into folklore. The old shops were built out of hard treacle-toffee or crushed battle-ships, they didn't invite you in, indeed you sometimes had the feeling you were *breaking* in, and the illusion that customer meant trespasser was reinforced when they charged you tuppence more than you'd have paid in a supermarket. There's just one thing, though – not only did they look different from the new shops, I think they were actually doing something different. Where they seemed to be catering – how-ever reluctantly, even spitefully – to what we needed, the new shops seem to be catering – with winsome efficiency – to what we crave.

We dived through the façade of the Great Gear Trading Company a bit like people jumping through a cinema screen and not expecting to find anything on the other side. But the interior was as colourful as the exterior, and there was an air of animation, not so much in the personnel or the clients as in the goods themselves. Perhaps animation isn't the right word, since it implies the organic – but then people who draw cartoons are called animators, they make inert things seem to move, and all I can say is the gear in the Great Gear Trading Company seemed to be jumping or twitching like a million fingers being tapped impatiently. You could buy dark glasses, yo-yos, personalized matchboxes, cigarette-papers, lucky joss-sticks, Mickey Mouse cushions, popguns, Union Jack waste-paper baskets, books that looked like books but weren't books (para-books, with titles like *Le Petomane, Fanny Hill's Cookbook, Private Eyesores, A Book of Bloomers*). There were large coloured surgical boots, or what looked like large coloured surgical boots, gramophone records in cardboard sleeves that were to be eaten on the spot rather than taken away, pink wax phalluses, electric back-scratchers, iron-on transfers, T-shirts *à choix*, old clo, comic posters, and badges proclaiming anything you had a mind to claim or pro-claim. In one corner there was a mass of kitchen equipment. I must be believed when I say that the imperma-nence of the context was so strong, so insistent, that all this kitchen equipment seemed instantly fictional; and a parallel sprang to mind.

Do you remember when *Mrs Dale's Diary* was trying to tell you it wasn't a de-boshed fairy tale but a true document? When it suddenly started to include – without at all varying its original idiom – a selection of the more operatic contingencies: rape, abortion, drugs; members of opposite sexes getting into bed together before the docket had been signed, even a hint that there were members of the same sex who might do the same thing, with much the same idea. The intention was to confer authenticity upon the fiction. But you know what actually happened – right, fiction was conferred upon authenticity, and people started feeling that sexual intercourse was as unbelievable as Mrs Dale's oft-repeated claim that she was worried about Jim. Well, that's the way the kitchen stuff at the Great Gear looked to me – it might as easily have grown wings and flown away as convince me you could take it home and cook with it. There's an outside chance I wasn't alone in feeling this, because when I went back to the Great Gear to remind myself that there was such a shop, the kitchen department had vanished. No one bought the stuff, because where everything else was a chimera, who was going to believe it?

But there's nobody so perverse as a middle-aged man in the presence of his mother. Feeling certain that the style of the place was likely to be unacceptable to her on the grounds of simple unfamiliarity, I staved off my own deeper feelings about it and began to recite a catalogue of its virtues. The colours were bright, the people were cheerfully dressed, the music made it sound like a party. I actually started doing a frantic irritated little dance in front of my mother, such as the middle-aged can sometimes be seen to do in the presence of the elderly, when they are mortally afraid that the elderly will not recognize that *their* attitudes are simple prejudice, whereas ours are based on reason. But my mother was as able as anyone else to accept that the shop's idiom was authentic, and she said yes, it was true, everything looked bright and new and young and so forth. But, she said, at the same time it makes me feel terribly depressed. And I said without a pause, So it does me. And my wife said, Me too. And we went our way, because the rain had stopped, and on and off ever since I've been wondering where the seat of the depression lies.

Of course it might be us, not the Great Gear. After all, we seek reflections of ourselves, and sometimes forego the true reflection for the frozen image which is merely prejudice – a symptom that we're unable to disentangle ourselves from the trammel of attitudes we once struck, which now have become stale and untruthful. Responses to which we cleave, precisely because we have stopped responding – stuck, so to speak, in a gramophone record of ourselves. But I discount this, on the admittedly rather jaunty grounds that if it were true I doubt if I'd be able to identify it. What I diagnose as the alienating factor in the Great Gear – and in all the other shops, painted on the air, two-dimensional, acryllic – is that while they deal in clothes and pizzas and yo-yos and coronation mugs, their dealings in what is impermanent are secondary to their dealings in what I take the true commodity to be – the *magic* of impermanence. They are not salesmen in these shops, they are adepts, they mediate impermanence. And the shops aren't shops, they're shrines inside which a single element has been extracted from the totality of experience, and – as in all primitive religions – is offered as the whole: impermanence becomes an avatar from which, if you're willing to make the sacrifice, redemption and surcease may be had – a promise that is endlessly unfulfilled, because endlessly unfulfillable.

Grottoes and bazaars are nothing new, but in the past, in the Gamages and the Lewises of another day, the instantly consumable was not separated from its contingent humanity, and intimations of permanence were supplied by three-piece suites. But now that even Harrods itself has a nonce-shop called Way-In, it's been necessary – to preserve the atmosphere of worship – to seal it off from the real world of the rest of the store, and the faithful ascend, completely insulated, in a special lift which stops nowhere else. And on arrival they enter, not another department, but another dimension. Through this dimension, the King's Road now principally winds, thronged with worshippers at the temple of the Great Gear, where the gospel of transience is preached, where people come not just to buy a funny poster for the loo but to swear fealty to the consumable. This is what lays a chill to the heart, here lies the frigid zone, which makes the Great Gear dry enough when it is raining, but never anything but cold.

Chestnuts

A friend of a friend of mine is a Bishop, and when he took over from the outgoing Bishop he thought the decent thing to do would be to invite the old chap back to dinner, especially since the way they arrange these things in the Church of England you not only get the superannuated Bishop's job, you get his palace as well. So the old Bishop returned to what had been his house, and he and his wife were entertained by his successor. They went into dinner and after the meal had ended, and the new Bishop was thinking things had gone off very well, the old Bishop turned to his wife and said, 'You know, my dear, we really are going to have to dismiss that cook.'

This sort of chestnut comes like a folksong from deep within the collective unconscious. It creates such a vivid picture that you can hardly believe you weren't present when it happened – but it didn't happen at all, it is part of an endless dream that we are all jointly dreaming. The dream has many mansions, in one of which there is a famous actor who (you remember) was very fond of drink, and came reeling on in *Richard III*, declaiming:

> Now is the wister of our dincontest
> Made glorious Yorkshire by the summer sun
> And all the cloused that loused upon our housed –

The audience started to mutter, and a voice shouted, 'You're drunk,' whereat the Duke of Gloucester (for it was he) swayed down to the footlights and cried, 'You're right – but just wait till you see the Duke of Buckingham.'

Perhaps it was *The Last of Mrs Cheyney* in which that great lady of the theatre Jean Forbes Robertson had some difficulty finding the right entrance, and the backcloth could be seen ballooning as she made her way uncertainly across, trying to fight her way through it on to the stage. At last she emerged, smiling rather glazedly. The other actors who had been waiting for her were sitting in frozen silence round a dining-room table, centre. Miss Forbes Robertson teetered up to them and with the same smile still on her face inquired, 'Why the fuck doesn't someone say something?' Stung, one of the other actors cried, 'Because it's your line, dear.' The curtain was rung down, and the manager appeared in front of it to explain that Miss Forbes Robertson was suffering from fish-poisoning.

This seems to have something in common with the occasion when Lady Ottoline Morrell (or Lady Sybil Colefax or Nancy Cunard, it scarcely matters which) saw in the course of one of her grand dinner-parties that the butler was drunk. Hastily, she scribbled a note and passed it to him. Unfolding it, he read the words, 'You are in a disgusting condition. Leave the room,' and swaying slightly he re-folded the paper and placed it in front of Sir John Simon.

These are poems, small and bright. As when an affectionate wife, seeing her husband's legs poking out from beneath the kitchen sink he appeared to be mending, bent down and tickled him privily. At which he jumped up, knocked himself unconscious against the sink and it turned out to be the plumber. When the ambulance men were called to carry him out on a stretcher, they were manoeuvring it down the stairs when someone explained how the accident had happened, and they laughed so heartily they let go of the handles and the plumber crashed down the stairs and broke his leg.

I wonder if it was the same lady who put a batch of scones in the oven, then went upstairs to her bath. Dipping her toe in the water, she decided it would be better if she turned the oven off, tripped down-stairs, *toute nue*, and went back into the kitchen. Hearing footsteps outside, she realized this must be the baker – a friendly soul whose habit was to walk straight in and put the bread on the table. Quick as a flash, she nipped into the broom-cupboard and closed the door. The footsteps walked in and across the kitchen floor, and the owner of the feet threw open the broom-cupboard door. It was the man to read the electricity meter: as he stared at the lady in the cupboard with no clothes on, she said – very reasonably, when you come to think about it – 'I was expecting the baker.'

These tales have a curious virtue. When you think about them days afterwards in a quiet moment, you burst out laughing.

Kidnapped

In a town in the south of France I was lunching with a French professor who had written a bestseller, and these days in France he is rather a star and people tend to recognize him. We were there to do some filming with him, and the director and the professor and I were sitting at a table on the terrace of the restaurant, and some way away at another table there sat a French woman with a face like a hand-made boot. Suddenly, she recognized the Prof, sailed across and cried, 'Oh you must all come and have a drink at my house.'

We murmured our regrets, how nice it would have been, but alas, there just wouldn't be time. 'Quite so,' the lady said, 'it is arranged. My house for drinks.' We stepped up our demurrers: it would have been fun, but time pressed, we had to fettle the camera, take the cosies off the microphones. 'We are just round the corner,' she declared, 'it will not take five minutes.' Ah, alas no. 'My house,' she said. 'I'll lead the way.' I raised my voice very slightly and said No. At this point the lady's son-in-law (one of those fat French not-so-young men, who look like capons) smoothly interposed – 'What is half an hour?' 'Well,' I said, and I was still struggling to keep an agreeable smile on my mush, though my whole face was beginning to feel like a windscreen that was shortly going to have to be replaced, 'that does rather depend which half-hour it is, really.' The son-in-law replied, 'No, it doesn't.' 'Oh, yes, it does,' I said, nodding gravely, which is quite hard to do when your voice seems to have gone awfully high. '*Le monsieur est si obstiné,*' hissed the Medusa, and she meant me, not her son-in-law, who to my by no means unjaundiced eye was looking more and more like a piece of fennel that had gone cold in brown sauce.

Well (*bref*, as the Froggies say), the monstrous woman won – she suborned the Prof, and then our director, and of course I had to go with them. 'She only wants to show us a little Gallic courtesy,' our director muttered, his natural innocence not uncut with malice, it seemed to me, on this occasion. 'Oh no, she doesn't,' I shouted, 'she wants to show us her furniture!' And I was right. I think there were eighteen rooms in her house and she spared us none, pricing every object in each. 'Why don't you make her an offer for the lot?' I said to our director, grinding my teeth, and the ancient besom, whose ear for imagined slights was as acute as her manners were grotesque, cried 'Nothing reproduction here – all authentic!'

When she struck the manacles off and we were out in the street at last, I stood in the sunshine and the steam coming out of my head obscured a distant view of Mont Blanc. Back in England, I said to a friend, Living as you do in East Molesey, could you imagine dashing out into the street and entangling three perfect strangers in your butterfly net and forcing them to come in and admire your G-plan? Funny you should say that, said my chum, I know some people who've just moved to East Molesey from Isleworth, and the last time I met them they said, 'We've got so many nice things in our house these days we don't invite people any more, it only makes them jealous.'

The PR Man

Mr Leslie Perrin is a cheerful man in his middle forties. He works from a small up-to-date office in Oxford Street, and on his wall, printed in a sans serif type and chastely framed, hangs the following legend: 'Public relations is the deliberate planned effort to establish and maintain mutual understanding between an organization and its public.'

Mr Perrin said, 'I bought five pounds of walnuts and spent the evening scooping out the kernels. I then dabbed clear Bostik round the tip of the shells, inserted the story and pressed them together again. Each walnut had a card hanging from it on a piece of thread. The card said, "HERE'S A STORY WORTH CRACKING."'

When Mr Perrin answers the telephone, he may greet his caller with the word 'Salutations'. In the course of conversation, and referring to the passage of time, he is apt to say 'Many moons'. He is a short, compact man, wistful and bonhomous, combining something of the physical appearance, and something of the mystery, of a small individual meat pie.

'I sincerely believe that PR does not begin and end with a large gin-and-tonic in the Wig and Pen Club. I very much believe that we in PR must offer a service. When it was a matter of launching the first news of Telstar, I put my head together with Mel Mark and Al Mark (Al is no relation of Mel's, Mel being a Swiss-based Mancunian) and we rendered the whole thing in human terms.'

The telephone rang, and Mr Perrin arranged for the Marquis of Bath to appear on a television programme.

'As I was saying, you either give a service, or you're a nothing person. Someone wanted me to publicize magnetic ashtrays for motor-cars, but he hadn't tumbled to the fact that they cover the metal with that mock-leather these days, so there's nothing for the ashtrays to stick to. I advised him against the scheme.'

Mr Perrin walked round his desk. 'I don't know if you've noticed that I've been keeping my hands in my pockets. That's because I gesticulate a lot. I suppose all Celtic peoples do.' Mr Perrin was born in Manchester, lives in London, but comes of Welsh stock.

'I went into PR on March 5, 1950. I think you'll find it was a Sunday. I used to do posters for Royal Baking Powder and Marshall's Master Mix, but that folded and I got a job in the Kangley Bridge Road painting LADIES and GENTS signs for use on the railways. It's quite a tricky business, the lettering. Anyway, after the Kangley Bridge Road, I started drawing seaside postcards –'

The telephone rang, and it was a client. Mr Perrin read over to him the profile he was proposing to circulate to the press – 'Jimmy used to help his father in the bakery, but the kind of dough Jimmy was set on making needed no crispy outside crust . . . October 2 is quite a date. It's the Feast of the Holy Angel Guardians, Aristotle the great Greek philosopher died on October 2, Richard III was born, and on October 2 it's Radio One with Jimmy Young . . . He's a helluva good man to have around the house when entertainment has to be woven into the flour-power of mid-morning cooking . . .' The client gave the words his imprimatur.

'Where was I? Yes, I did these postcards for a very lovely delightful man, but unfortunately the police caught him with several bales of uncouponed suit material, and that ended the connection. I became a clerk at Dorking North, on what was then the Southern Railway, auditing the accounts of all stations from K to L – Knockholt, Lancing, Ladywell, I audited them all. Subsequently I joined the Control

Commission in Germany and drew graphs under that very charming person Lady Charlotte Bonham-Carter. They were graphs of – what's that word for measuring food –' Mr Perrin put his head into the outer office '– Pat, what's that word for – of course, calories. We circulated these calorie graphs to embassies throughout the world.

'Then I got a job on the *Melody Maker*, teaching people how to hold the maracas correctly. My wife posed with two forks, and I'd do an instructional sketch. I did a bit of band work after that, though I was better at the chatting, getting the dates and arranging the money, than playing the drums. PR seemed the natural step.'

Mr Perrin paced the floor, and glanced into his bookshelf. 'I read a lot, you know. Psychology and the bending of personality. Books on primitive government. It lets me know what's going on.' He stared hard at a book called *The Spirit of Scotland*, as though wondering how it had crept in. 'And although I'm not going to deny that I was once arraigned before the justices at Nottingham for scattering leaflets from an aeroplane on the subject of a band I was then promoting, I can honestly say I don't pull stunts any more. I've grown out of them. As I say, unless you've got a purpose in life, you're a nothing individual.'

Mr Perrin said he liked people. 'But I can't be sycophantic. I'm not given to be a sycophant. I just can't do it. Maybe I don't show my dislike of somebody, but that's simple courtesy. I cultivate friends in Fleet Street because we speak the same language, but although you live by your contacts, I refuse to be insincere.'

More telephoning, then; 'PR is the easiest thing in the world to get into. All you need is a telephone, and I'm the first to agree that some public relations men can't even type, let alone write. But you must realize that all professions – dentistry, hypnotism, psychiatry – have their quacks, and I can assure you the only thing I would like to be known as is a good PRO. To me, this is terribly serious.'

Mr Perrin prepared to leave for Fleet Street, after showing me a gift he had brought back from his travels and which he was going to present to one of the lady journalists. It was a wax model of a girl in a bikini, and when you took her head off, there was a bottle inside.

My Leg in His Mouth

I was walking across a footbridge over the Kingston By-pass and, as I went down the steps on the other side, I saw a lady and a boy and a big black dog coming up towards me. The dog seemed to spot me and crossed over to the side of the steps I was going down. As he got nearer, I thought maybe I'd better move over. Then I thought, 'No, dammit, he's only a dog, let him move over.' The next thing I knew he'd got my leg in his mouth.

I said, 'My goodness. Goodness me. Crumbs.' Then, the three of us – and the dog, of course – stood looking at each other, none of us quite knowing what the appropriate response might be. Then the lady, as though she'd suddenly had a good idea – and I must say I applauded it – turned round and welted the dog round the mazard for about a minute and a half. But that was OK by the dog, he'd had his bite and, as I looked at it pretending to hang its head, I knew it knew I knew you couldn't get a dog to unbite you.

I felt awfully angry but, since the dog couldn't understand English, there wasn't any point in telling it anything and I couldn't say much to the woman since after all *she* hadn't bitten me. But I felt I was entitled to some sort of complaint and I looked at the hole in my trousers and cried aloud, 'Well, you can buy me another pair.' And the woman said, her voice rising to match mine, 'Have I said I won't?' And for a second or two it was touch and go whether I wasn't going to apologize to her: I even started to try to soothe her. Then I thought, 'Here, hold on. It's you the dog bit.' And the next thing I said was, 'Waist 38, inside leg 29, the next time you're in Marks and Spencers you can buy me some.' And she said anxiously, 'Are you sure they're navy blue?'

At this, for reasons I can't quite fathom, but probably because I felt he wasn't playing his part, I rounded on the small boy and shouted, 'You can remember the measurements.' 'Yes, yes,' he shouted back, 'I will.' 'All right,' I said threateningly, 'what are they?' 'Waist 38, inside leg 29,' he responded – and I suddenly thought, 'What on earth am I doing getting a perfect stranger to shout out my inside leg measurements in the wilderness of the Kingston By-pass?'

All very unsatisfactory, and I can only say that the faintly surreal air that the whole event carried was endorsed when I took my purple mumbled leg into St Stephen's Hospital to have an anti-tetanus injection and found myself thinking that the doctor who supervised this delicate operation looked exactly like a schoolgirl on the television programme *Ask the Family*, only to have her tell me that that was where I'd met her, ten years before.

Non Sequitur

I dearly love a non sequitur if it's operatic enough, and, marooned overnight in the city of Washington, I turned on the television and caught the opening lines of one of the commercials. The scene was a bus-stop and it was raining, and the man standing there with his umbrella turned to the camera and said, 'In weather like this, diarrhoea's no fun.' For sheer quality, no programme was going to match that, so I turned it off and went to bed.

How Not to Write Books

The first book I didn't write was my autobiography. When the letter arrived asking for it, I wasn't altogether surprised. I was nineteen and spending a good deal of time in public libraries looking at *Who's Who* to see if anyone had sneaked my name in without telling me. I showed the letter to my mother and she said, 'Have you done enough?' I reminded her of the time I was had up for riding a motorbike without tax, licence, insurance, audible warning of approach, brakes or lights. 'Then there was the letter I wrote to the *Wimbledon Boro News* when they wanted to pull the lamp-posts down.

Pretty ironic stuff. And what about the time your grandfather ran out into the road when Queen Victoria was going by and clapped her on the cheeks and said, "God Bless Your Old Chops"?'

'No, that was your dad's grandfather,' my mother said. 'My grandfather used to stand up before plays began and make the audience sing "Three Cheers for the Red, White and Blue".'

Everyone thinks they're special, so if anything comes your way looking remotely like evidence, that's what you take it for. I dropped a line to the autobiography people saying I was open to offers. They wrote back saying good, there were two courses open to me: I could send them £600 and they'd publish anything I cared to supply them with, or on the other hand I could take their special three-month course at the usual fees. I knew all along it was going to turn out like that, but when she saw my face my mother felt so sorry for me she bought me a pair of green corduroys.

The next thing was I started dreaming I'd written books and waking up and finding I hadn't. I remember waking up one cold morning on the floor of my girlfriend's digs in Sheffield and yelling, 'I've done it,' before I realized I'd only dreamt it. 'I don't know what the title was, but it was a Penguin, a lovely orange one, I could smell the print.' It was like those dreams you have when you're a child and you dream someone's given you a toy motorcar that can fly, and you wake up and it isn't even Saturday. I had another dream that kept recurring, about having written half a book, half a book that I'd forgotten about, and there it was with my name on it, bound in with half a book written by someone else. I've heard of some miserable ambitions, but never one to beat dreaming you've written half a book.

This dream came in instalments, and sometimes I'd be walking into the publishers trying to find out how the MS had got into their hands, trying to remember when I'd written it, and never being able to put my finger on what the damn thing was about. Sometimes I dreamt I was in a bookshop not being able to find it and thinking in the dream I must have dreamt it. I remember L. A. G. Strong telling us at school how he didn't mind having reveries about being President of the United States, but if he started doing the same thing about writing enormously successful books, he'd know his last hour as a novelist had struck.

So all these books got away, didn't exist, and after I'd been a journalist for a bit another one followed them. This was going to be called *Oxford Bags – Whoops!* At least, that was the tentative title the publisher had given it in the letter he wrote saying I was the only man for the job. But every time I sat down and thought about it, I generated the wrong sort of reminiscence: the publisher was after the sound of broken glass and girls being smuggled out of Magdalen in laundry-baskets, but I kept conjuring up terribly literal tableaux, like the time a man called Young tipped a plate of sausage, beans and chips into his lap at the Lyons in Cornmarket Street. He leant on it with his elbow and it turned right over. He just sat looking down at the beans running into his turn-ups and I think he was on the verge of tears. We were all very interested in food in those days – that's to say we liked it copious and cheap – and Young had actually paid for and was looking forward to eating an extra portion of the beans. 'I'll always be one —ing dinner down,' he said quietly, when he'd got control of himself, 'and, as you all know, I was proud of the trousers.'

Everything I remember about Oxford is rather like that, very distinct and totally irrelevant. How could I put in about Davies, who is now a clergyman, drinking a bottle of Worcester sauce? Bottle of madeira, yes, or a three-pint sconce, but there's no resonance in Worcester sauce. It takes a bit of doing, and he did it all right, I think it was one of the most convincing displays of fortitude I've ever seen, but you couldn't call it showy.

And that was the trouble, I couldn't remember the glamorous side of things: it had sunk through my experience like water through sand, and all that was left behind were lugubrious epiphanies. Me walking out of L M H after time and, in some confused way, thinking to deceive the porteress into believing I was a plumber: 'The Moabs is atrocious,' I shouted hoarsely and I pulled my cap down over my eyes, and she replied – how it makes my cheeks burn to remember – 'Rubbish, you silly boy.' I was tethered to the humdrum, the witty dinners at Woodstock had all gone under the hill, and I recalled a gloomy back-room at a café near Carfax, and one undergraduate saying to another, 'Well lend us tuppence, then, just so I'll have something to jingle.'

I think it's being asked to do the books that stuns my imagination. I've read books by telly men that make the act of talking into a camera sound like something out of *Last Year at Marienbad*, but when a publisher wanted me to do the same sort of thing I was pegged down to the earth of my own conviction that doing television was as unmysterious as it looked, i.e. you decided what you wanted to say, pointed yourself at the camera, and said it. What I was short on was tight corners and tricky situations. Or perhaps it was vanity, not wanting your life to be diminished to the moments when you happened to be sitting next to someone who'd taken it into his head to alarm old ladies by repeating the forbidden word, or when you happened to be in the same Lime Grove lav with a Prime Minister and he looked at the amenities and said, 'I say, it's rather grand.'

So I didn't, and I don't think I ever will, because the books publishers ask you to write are the ones they ought to invent machines to manufacture: fashion-mongering nonce-books, about television or eating well or snobbery or dukes or all the trendy people. So it's not really the books that get away, it's me. Off like a shot straight after the pudding, the tendons all knotting down the side of the neck that was turned towards the publisher who had been standing me the lunch, the neck that is poorer by about two thousand nods, all done sideways, the most punishing sort of nod, ten years' nodding squeezed into an hour and a quarter, nods that didn't nourish the nodder because they were all a preface to saying no. And as I turn into Romilly Street, there's only one thing that bothers me: while I'm too proud to write a book that is only a commodity, I appear to be too idle to write one that could be described as anything else.

Body-fascism [sic]

Anna Ford the speakerine struck her own tiny blow for the calcification of language. Getting up at a meeting of some narcissistic female society or other, she complained – apparently without any intention of amusing – that there weren't enough plain women in television, a wretched state of affairs she blamed on men, who tended to hire the good-lookers rather than the traffic wardens. This syndrome she described as 'body-fascism'. I couldn't help thinking that if, when Anna Ford makes up the words for herself, she can precipitate such a stone-in-the-kidney as 'body-fascism', then we've got rather more to thank the men who compose the news for her and write it up in nice big letters so she can read it out than perhaps we'd realized.

According to Miss Ford, the newspapers are obsessed with her body. 'I meet eminent men,' she says, 'who tell me, "I am not listening to the news when you read it. I am just looking at you."'

I think this speaks rather well for the eminent men. There they all are – fast-food franchisers, deckchair attendants, Sir Geoffrey Howe – doesn't it occur to Miss Ford they're just being *polite*? Apparently not. When she hears their compliments she says, 'I just feel I'm not doing my job properly.' She could try doing it with a bag over her head. Sandy Gall does, and is thus spared all those perfumed hussies who would otherwise be tearing at his rich suitings. But what puzzles me is the logic. If she resents the possibility that she got the job because she's good-looking, why did she take it? Why didn't she say, 'I've got this old dog of an aunty with a poke bonnet and two large warts – why don't you try her?' Well, maybe aunty *was* asked, but stuck to her knitting on the grounds that compared to reading out short words in capital letters, knitting put her on nodding terms with Heidegger. What really does beat cockfighting is the way people who are on public show start to believe that mere publicity transforms you into a sage. If I were a newsreader, I hope I'd have the sense to read the bulletins, and in between keep my pretty mouth shut.

Fourth Person Singular

Of course, they are men of special distinction, and if they hadn't been, we wouldn't have gone: but because the eminence of Alberto Moravia and Heinrich Böll can be taken for granted, it leaves you relaxed enough to be simply curious. I found I was looking forward to seeing Moravia, partly to scoop him for *The Book Programme*, and partly to confirm an impression I had had for years that he looks exactly like Mr Griffiths who used to run a chemist's shop in Motspur Park.

We drove out to Moravia's summer place, a little seaside spot to the south of Rome, a bit like Angmering, scrubby and blowy, the villas strung out on the *lungomare* with that special air of not belonging, of having been manufactured elsewhere, which you find in houses along by-pass roads. And when we got there, I saw that Moravia not only looked like Mr Griffiths, he had the same slightly halting walk, the same address – unemphatic, unemotional, vaguely fierce. With a dispassion Griffiths used to reserve for charging you a penny or two more than Boots, Moravia corrected my assumption that the stories in his collection *Lady Godiva* were told in the female first person: no, he said, they were told in the female fourth person. To the three conventional pronouns he had added another, an 'I' separated from the original 'I' for the purpose of keeping that 'I' under observation and telling the story. 'This dimension of self-consciousness is new in life as well as in art. Once, people would do what they did without bothering to know what it was they were doing. Now they know what they're doing, but,' he added impassively, 'they go on doing it.'

Moravia believes in the connection between sex and creativity just as strongly as the hero of his novel *The Two of Us* – the story of a man who is tyrannized by his own phallus, and is in a continual state of struggle with his intransigent member in the hope of sublimating the animal drive and turning it into art. 'But,' says Moravia, 'like the man in the book, most people believe they have sublimated when, in fact, all they have done is repress.' This is about the only funny book Moravia has written, and he based the theme (though it crops up in folklore) on the habit of Roman youths who, especially in moments of sexual stress, address their members by name: 'Ah, Giovanni, thou hast failed me, truly this is a betrayal.'

It is curious the way one physical resemblance seems to guarantee another. Mr Griffiths was deaf – so is Moravia. But, at this point, the parallels started to extend from the man to the métier: the picture in my head of Mr Griffiths transferring a small bottle from a shelf to the counter – something he would do with great economy of movement, a movement that was the exact opposite of a flourish – seemed at the same time an image of that peremptoriness with which, in his stories, Moravia discloses the matter to the reader. Both actions have about them the implication that, although life is mostly a slew of loose ends, here, at least, is a transaction that is conclusive – save for one thing: you have to pay. I do not see Mr Griffiths writing novels (though there may yet be a pile of manuscripts to be discovered), but I do see Moravia running a chemist's shop: a faintly threatening one, lit by the sort of light which throws no shadows. And now I think of it, his stories are like prescriptions.

I don't know why I have this impulse to convert the public and institutional into the domestic and familiar. I carried an image of Böll with me when I went to see him at Cologne – it was a shot from the news film taken at the time of Solzhenitsyn's expulsion from Russia. He had gone to stay with Böll at his cottage in the German countryside, and, in this shot of the house, the reporters were clustered about in the small front garden, and Böll was leaning out of an upstairs window telling them, in a kindly way, that if they were patient, Solzhenitsyn would do his best to supply them with whatever it was they wanted. I suppose it was the homeliness of the upstairs window that conferred the humanity on this little exchange – that, and Böll's face, which is nothing if not parental: yes, his receiving countenance seemed to telegraph to the journalists, the children could have another five minutes to play. Well, this fantasy of the man was not too wide of the mark. Böll told me that when he heard Solzhenitsyn was coming, his first feeling was one of relief that the builders had finished the inside lavatory – what with the cottage being thoroughly rural, they'd only had the privy at the end of the garden, it was a mercy they had at last decided to have the thing done properly, nothing wrong with the outside one, indeed, it had a pretty wooden door with a heart-shaped motif, but, well, would it have been quite the thing to offer a visitor of such renown, not that Solzhenitsyn would have minded, since, as well as being a very ascetic man, he is also a very humorous man, a first-class mime – but, well, after all, one would not have felt comfortable.

I laughed, and so did he. When I watched the arrival of Solzhenitsyn on the telly, I was wondering about just that sort of thing. To those of us with our noses pushed up against the screen, it was a scenario – one world-famous reputation receiving another. But those involved were obliged to meet as people. This must have entailed choosing the right pyjamas to lend the guest, finding out whether he took jam or marmalade for breakfast, tiptoeing past his bedroom in case he wanted to sleep late, while he lay awake inside wondering if it was too early to get up. Böll's first gift to Solzhenitsyn was a pencil and an exercise book. Then they spoke of the importance of a clean shirt to a man in gaol. For preference, it should be white, soft, nicely ironed. These details acted on me as the commonplace furniture of the world acts on the people in Böll's stories: I was consoled by the strangeness of the ordinary.

Böll had been reading *Humboldt's Gift*, Saul Bellow's novel, and told me he had been instrumental in first getting Bellow published in Germany. The publisher had been doubtful, but Böll had shamed him into it. I remember asking Bellow in an interview if he had ever been curious to visit the places in Russia his family had come from. Yes, he had, he told me, but he had only got as far as Warsaw. Arriving in Warsaw, he found so much there to remind him of his family background, he felt he needn't go further. In Warsaw, there were the churches, and the wall-hangings, and the tea-drinking ceremonies, and somehow Warsaw had all the ingredients of a familiar mystery. What Bellow said was committed to film, and, when I got the transcript back from the typist, I saw a magician had been at work. For Warsaw, the transcript read Walsall throughout. I never think of this without feeling grateful.

But not all magic is of the white variety. I refused money to a gypsy in Rome, and when I later saw her climbing into a Mercedes on her way to see the Pope, I felt a glow of triumph. But as she drove past, she cursed me, and on that instant I lost all my traveller's cheques, the battery of the car we had hired – from Avis, natch – went flat during the rush hour in the Piazza Barberini, an aeroplane flew away from Rome airport leaving us behind because the departure had never been announced, and the gum on the labels you identify cans of film with lost all virtue and refused to stick. Somehow the curdling of the gum was the most convincing demonstration of the gypsy's power. I hailed a passing Jesuit, crammed money into his scrip, and begged him to found an orphanage. But the Old Religion was still working like a charm: the plane home was abruptly cancelled owing to fog at Stuttgart (a climatic novelty unheard of at this time of year), and, as I type these words, news comes that the *middle* roll of the three rolls of film which carry my interview with Heinrich Böll is inexplicably out of focus, though the cameraman had not touched the lens. I just hope when that gypsy arrived at Castelgandolfo, the Pope crossed her palm with silver, because, if he didn't, the next time we see him he'll have been changed into the Archbishop of Canterbury.

Being Rude

When someone's deliberately rude to you, you can hardly believe it. As when a complete stranger at a party joined the group I was in and after a bit, baring his teeth in a smile that anticipated the pleasure he was going to give himself, said to me in a high clear voice, 'How *unctuous* you are,' turned his back, and walked away. I nearly burst into tears. Then there was a waiter in a restaurant long ago who when I asked for the manager simply stared at me stonily and said, 'He wouldn't come.'

For a second the whole world crackles with malice, is lit up by a sinister glow that is not without a dangerous warmth. But there is another sort of rudeness that turns life down so that it is a fraction of a degree colder, and people are helped to stay away from each other in a climate of endless mutual disregard. I'm thinking of daily encounters where the negative possibilities are the only possibilities the two parties are interested in. You're looking for an inner tube, a sheet of plate glass, a music-centre, a place to park, an evening paper, floor tiles, a typewriter ribbon, and the really awful thing isn't that the man stares through you, it's the way you've come along prepared to stare through *him* – long before he refuses to acknowledge *you*, you have been ready not to acknowledge him simply because this is the response you expected. And when he shakes his head but doesn't say anything, or says 'No' and doesn't add the words 'I'm sorry', you turn away, and just because you're determined to give him even less than he gives you, you force yourself not to say 'Thank you'. Walking away from the bleak moonscape of one of these encounters – was it a doormat I wanted, planning permission, change for the telephone? – I realized it wasn't him I was damaging, it was me. I'd let his coldness prescribe my own, and in turning up with my refrigerator already on, had done my little bit to ensure that his would be in perfect working order. The icecap of anomie is spreading, so I make a vow to smile and say 'Please' and 'Thank you' and 'Goodbye', irrespective of what anyone else does, and it is a self-interested decision, for I know that the ritual of the smile will protect me, not from his resentment, but from my own.

At the same time, I wish there was the slightest chance of my ever plucking up courage to use a foreign language phrase-book I have on my shelves, which is written in the traditional stilted idiom of such guides, the only difference being that every single phrase is abusive – indeed, the book's sub-title is *How to be Abusive in Five Languages*. At the laundry, for example, you are advised to open rhetorically with the disobliging inquiry 'Don't you use soap?' and follow up this thrust with the words 'I suspect your dirty staff have been wearing my shirts.' At the beach you may endear yourself to your neighbour by saying 'Move your fat carcase so I can get some sun' (*'Eh, gros! Enleve-toi de mon soleil.'*), remarking cordially to the beach attendant, 'These deck-chairs look as though they are covered in dog muck.' Swinish at the beach, you pick quarrels in bars by saying to the barman, 'When you've sobered up, perhaps you'll bring me a drink,' and when it comes you ask him, 'Is it your general practice to water the beer?' On arrival at the theatre you find someone in your seat and you cry threateningly, 'Move your fat arse,' and once you have settled in you inquire in a loud voice, 'Is this supposed to be an amateur performance?'

At a restaurant afterwards you maintain your reputation for wit by asking genially, 'Do you keep pigs in here between meals?' or possibly, 'Are indigestion tablets served with every course?' Blundering back to your hotel, you observe pleasantly to the desk clerk, 'I suppose you have been letting my room by the hour while I've been out,' and having called for the bill and read it you ask, 'Are you sure you haven't added in the date?' Picking up your bags you leave, turning at the door to say, 'Congratulations, your hotel has the biggest fleas in Europe.'

Simple abuse can be very refreshing, but most of us don't have the courage and mask hostility by straining after subtlety. We go in for pale imitations of the odious Mr Bennet in *Pride and Prejudice* ('Thank you, my dear' to his daughter at the piano, 'you have delighted us long enough'), when what we'd really like to be able to do is clap someone on the back and cry, 'Talking of sewers, how's your father?'

Washing the Wigs

A slightly surreal experience stays with me. I contrived to enter the apartment of a publisher in Paris by way of the cellars – looking back, this must have taken a bit of doing, but at the time I saw no other way in, and concluded the man forced his visitors to pass through a sort of hulks that dripped like Wapping Old Stairs, and then ascend in a sort of dumb-waiter designed to hold garbage, in obedience to some interior-decorator's whim. But of course I'd just got it wrong, and when I fell out of the dumb-waiter into the kitchen I was greeted by a manservant in black trousers and green apron who – no doubt to distract me from my embarrassment – resorted to general topics, and said in a kindly way – or at least I thought he said – 'I have just been washing the wigs.' Shaking the cabbage stalks out of my turn-ups, I followed him to the drawing-room, wondering if he meant his own wig and that of his employer. Or was it that his employer had many wigs, one perhaps for each day of the week? Would they be steaming in front of the drawing-room fire? My host laughed politely when he heard of my odd entry, no doubt supposing that in entering via the waste-disposal unit I had been exercising a peculiarly English form of humour. My mind running on the wig problem, I suddenly wondered if it wasn't the word 'peruke' I'd heard but the word '*perroquets*' – perhaps what the man had said was 'I have just been washing the parrots.' This seemed even less likely until I looked down and saw one of these amiable birds shambling towards me over the Aubusson. It looked purposefully at me, hopped on to my knee, and whistled the Marseillaise from first note to last. When I told someone about these events, he simply said, 'No, not parrot – parakeet,' as though this was the only bit that interested him. But when I left the apartment, I felt I was walking out of a picture by Magritte or Delvaux.

Ivy

I'm not sure whether the word *was* a misprint or not, but in an article about Ivy Compton Burnett I think they meant to say the word 'books' when they said 'Her books are as perfect as pieces of music – you couldn't improve them.' But what actually got printed was 'Her *looks* are as perfect as pieces of music – you couldn't improve them.' As I say, it might not be a misprint, but when you recall that Dame Ivy looked like Austen Chamberlain wearing a bird's nest, there is room for doubt.

H-Certificate

I was reading about a government report in the *Daily Telegraph*, and noted with some concern that the report – according to the writer of the article – had turned out to be a 'damp squid'. This was because (said the writer) they didn't want to rock the boat. But damp squids are noted for rocking boats. I thought there was a good story by Kafka going to waste there – chap in the Min. of Ed. reaches into the file and touches these awful tentacles. Vincent Price for the title role.

B. Traven:
A Mystery Solved

The aim of the investigation was to crack a literary conundrum that had foxed everyone who'd ever tried their hand at it – to the world of letters it was the equivalent of the Colonel Fawcett mystery, and many a grizzled critic and many a saddleworn don had set off up this particular Amazon to find their man, and all had returned from a jungle of misdirection, false trails, Indian signs and tiger traps to explain that they hadn't actually *found* anyone but they'd heard rumours: that the man was an American millionaire, that he was Jack London, that he was a German prince, a Negro slave, and even the last President of Mexico but three. Our own expedition, fully provisioned with the previous literature, and armed to the teeth with the man's actual works, set forth with modest expectations, but we got lucky. Three quarters of the way through impenetrable savannahs of identity, we picked up a spoor. Breaking into a trot, next into a run, we burst into a clearing – and found him. But I was there first . . .

It all began one evening in a bookshop. Wandering round the shelves with a friend I picked up a paperback. It was called *The Bridge in the Jungle*, and the author's name was one that had always sounded a note that was strange: B. Traven. I said, 'Traven. Let's find him.' My companion said, 'Who's Traven?' and I said, 'That's the point – no one knows.' I went to the cash desk and I bought the book. I hadn't read a line of the man's works, but there are certain books you haven't read that exercise a stronger grip on your imagination than many you know by heart.

Whoever B. Traven was, he manufactured his anonymity so carefully that he might have been as fictional as the novels he produced. His books sell in their millions, particularly in America and in Eastern Europe, but no actual physical presence, no single individual, had ever claimed to have written them. There wasn't a publisher who had ever met Traven, no agent came forward willing to introduce his client. The name Traven was on the books, but the man Traven never signed his name, he typed it. The letters arriving in publishers' offices, and purporting to come from Traven, were inflexible in their prohibition of biographical details: dust-jackets were to be left blank, and the writer would have preferred it if his name had been left off the title-page. Nobody knew in what language the stories had originally been composed, nobody knew in what country the author had been born, indeed nobody knew if Traven was one man or several. But what's clear is that in absenting himself in this curiously complete way, Traven became more real rather than less. In the absence of humdrum flesh and blood, he became legendary, and it was even said that those who went in search of him were mysteriously destroyed, like men in fairy-tales.

We decided to risk it. My companion in the bookshop was Will Wyatt, a television producer with whom I had often worked. Like mendicant friars we shuffled the corridors of the BBC begging money for the expedition, advertised for seasoned researchers who had no fear of the telephone, and embarked for Mexico. This romantic destination was the one fixed element in the Traven story, for though nothing else was known about the provenance of the manuscripts, Mexico was the country from which someone had posted them.

By this time the zest I felt for the chase had been underpinned by something more substantial, my reading of the books themselves. Traven had written a dozen novels as well as many short stories, awkwardly expressed fables that have an imaginative grip that rivals 'The Ancient Mariner'. Indeed, his first published novel is a tale of the sea that exudes a paranoia reminiscent of Coleridge's poem – placelessness and anomie dog the hero of *The Death Ship*, another Flying Dutchman who is doomed to wander the world stoking the boilers of a hulk, without papers, without identity. The world affronts Traven in its treatment of the individual, as his stories of the Mexican Indian clearly show.

On our arrival in Mexico our first witness, living in the seaside resort of Puerto Viarta, was John Huston, whose film *The Treasure of the Sierra Madre* had been based on Traven's novel of the same name: a classic study of the corrosive effect of greed. Huston spoke of Traven's quality as a writer in the following words:

'He was a very passionate and eloquent writer, a defender of the victims of society. He hated injustice, and God knows he found a great

battlefield here in Mexico. The vision was so great . . . and that's what
Traven had – a great vision. The books are all marvellous affirmations
of his faith in the beaten man.'

No one had ever spoken of meeting Traven, but one night in Mexico
City, while Huston was preparing the shooting-script of the *Sierra
Madre*, he heard a sound in his hotel room in the early hours of the
morning:

'I woke up and someone was standing at the foot of my bed. I sat
up in bed and said, "Hello." He took out a card and gave it to me
– just shortly after daylight this was. I read the card. It said "Hal
Croves – translator, Acapulco and San Antonio". After I'd read the
card, he gave me a letter, and the letter was signed "B. Traven". The
letter said that he, Traven, was ill, and that in his stead he was sending
his intimate friend, Hal Croves. And that anything that I could have
got from himself, Croves could furnish me.'

Croves is just about as strange a name as Traven: it has an anagram-
matic quality that suggests the absence of anyone real. Why would
Traven have so intimate a confidant? Croves knew so much he might
well have been Traven himself:

'Croves expressed the same thoughts that Traven had, and the
thought crossed my mind, could this possibly *be* Traven? I told Traven
– I told Croves – of certain changes that I intended to make, and he
listened and nodded. He was obviously an old Mexico hand.'

When the film got under way, Croves was a constant bystander. He
came each day and watched intently. It was noticed that he avoided
the stills photographer, but he was snapped once, unawares. When the
film was finished, Croves disappeared. Huston said that this was the
last he saw of the man, he went away, and they never corresponded.
But Huston had relinquished his early suspicion that Croves might
have been Traven. To Huston, the man Croves – diminutive, socially
maladroit, in his baggy shorts almost a figure of fun – could surely not
be Traven, a writer whose obsessive self-assurance was his hallmark.
But who was Croves?

In his way he was as elusive as Traven, as one of his friends who
is still living in Mexico City discovered. This was the distinguished
cinematographer Gabriel Figueroa. Figueroa's sister-in-law, Esperanza Lopez Mateos, had become Traven's agent, though of course she
had never met Traven himself, only the man who explained that he
was Traven's translator – Hal Croves. On one occasion she had

arranged to meet Croves in a café in Mexico City. But Miss Lopez Mateos was ill and Gabriel Figueroa went in her place:

'So I went over to the café, and there was Mr Croves sitting with his cup of coffee, waiting, and a few customers around. So I get close and say, "Are you Mr Croves?" He turns, looks at me and says, "No." So what can I do? No telephone in the café, so I had to go out to find a telephone and tell Esperanza that probably I was mistaken or something. She says, "No, no, he is the man you are describing." So I go back and he was not there any more.'

This was some time in the forties, and a little while later Croves was gone. He had left Mexico City. But now for the first time someone was planning an assault on Traven, someone had decided that he would hunt B. Traven down and give him a face. It was a Mexican journalist called Luis Spota. These days Spota is a great whiz on Mexican television, but at the time Croves disappeared from Mexico City Spota was a callow 22-year-old reporter and, as he himself is the first to say, none too scrupulous. Spota had a chum who worked in a bank, and it was a casual word from this man that started things off. The friend said there was an account in the bank under the name B. Traven Torsvan. This added a further name to a growing list, but Spota's friend thought it might be a clue. Spota was delighted:

'I went to the bank, made some moves, not always legal – but we are reporters anyway – and I get a small short-cut to this box. And in this box I found some interesting material, especially a letter in the name of M. L. Martinez, a very common name in Mexico, with an address – Post Office 49 – in Acapulco.'

Getting leave of his editor, Spota took off for Acapulco and homed in on the post office:

'So one day a lady, dark lady, Mexican lady, young, went to the post office, take the letters. I follow her. I know exactly the address of her house – Cashew Park – something like a big beer garden. In that place, Maria de la Luz Martinez was living with an American – we suppose he was an American – named Berick Torsvan. He was a very small man, thin man, blond man, shy man.'

Straight away Spota was convinced that this man Torsvan, who was the owner of a roadside café and small-holding, was B. Traven. Posing as a tourist, Spota began to make a habit of dropping in at the café:

'This man – who has, by the way, twenty-five dogs always with him

when he comes and when he leaves the place – came spontaneously
to my table to drink the same lemonade, and he start with me a nice
friendship. He told me he was living in Mexico since long time ago,
and he told me the first thing that convinced me I was in the good
direction. He told me a story of two men in the south of Mexico who
fought with machetes until one of them killed the other and the other
dies, too. It was one of the stories in one of Traven's books.'

Spota returned to Mexico City and started a search in government
offices for the immigration card he was confident he would find in
Torsvan's name, and sure enough there it was. The name was on
record as Traven Torsvan, and the birthplace was down as Chicago.
Returning to the poste-restante number at the post office in Acapulco,
Spota bribed one of the clerks and with his assistance laid hands on
a letter addressed to Torsvan from Gabriel Figueroa.

'I make a friend in the post office, and I am a little indiscreet, and
we have a great curiosity – and we open the letter from Gabriel
Figueroa. We make a copy, a photostatic copy. Well, when I think
I have enough proof against him, I tell him, "I think you are B.
Traven." And his reaction was, he was very upset. And then later he
got very quickly angry. He put his hand very violently on the table
and told me, "You are a son of a bitch." And he left the table with
his twenty-five dogs.'

But the next day Spota turned up again at the tea-garden and the man
called Torsvan denied the charge in elaborate and contradictory detail:

'And he said, "You are wrong because I am not B. Traven, I am his
cousin." He told me, "Well, Mr Traven is dead. He dies many years
ago." Later he told me Traven is sick of tuberculosis. The other day
he told me that he was able to pay me, to give me some money in order
to keep me silent, and I tell him, "I don't care about money. I don't
want your money because *you* are my goal. B. Traven is my goal, my
challenge. I want to be a very good reporter." I was then twenty-two
years old. And he say – I don't remember when, this day or this night
– "You are going to be responsible for the death of a man if you publish
your story in your magazine *Mañana*. I am going to kill myself and
you are going to have over your conscience my death." Then I said,
"Well, that's your choice, that's your problem, not mine." I was very
cynical then. And I published the story and by good fortune for the
literature in the world and for humanity, he did not kill himself.'

No doubt about it, Spota had worked like a beaver, and all this foot-in-door stuff earned him a prize for investigative reporting. But a month after his articles had appeared in *Mañana*, the editor received a letter from Traven. It came from England, where Traven claimed to be living. Spota was dubious:

'I took the paper to the Technological Institute of Mexico. And we discovered this: the paper was Mexican, the ink of the typewriter was Mexican, the glue of the envelope was Mexican.'

As the reader might expect, Torsvan disappeared from Acapulco. And as the reader might also guess, Croves re-emerged in Mexico City. It is plain from the photographs that exist that Croves and Torsvan were the same man. And all Croves's documents were in the name of Traven Torsvan. But to show that Torsvan was Croves is not the same as showing that either of them was Traven.

As Huston recollects, people who assumed Croves was Traven, and used the name Traven in his presence, were mercilessly snubbed:

'Occasionally, someone would come up, some brash person, and ask him directly and rudely, "Are you B. Traven?" And when that happened in my presence I'd flinch. I never asked him that question, by the way.'

Sanora Babb Howe, widow of the famous Hollywood cameraman James Wong Howe, and a friend of Croves, committed the same solecism:

'One day, when we were talking about one of Traven's books, I made the mistake of referring to him as Traven. And he didn't say ust then, but he left soon after that – not in any anger – and came back and put a note under my door. The note was a personal note about that I must understand that he was absolutely not Traven, and I mustn't address him in this way. And it seemed to me if he weren't, he really wouldn't have to give that elaborate excuse. The next day he came again and asked me if I had got the note. And I said yes. And he asked if he could have it, and he tore it up.'

Figueroa was a great friend, and Croves had the use of a room in Figueroa's house. But then Figueroa did not allow himself to question his friend's identity, punctiliously avoiding the name Traven. To Figueroa the man was always Hal or even Mr Croves. Lawrence Hill, who published some of Traven's Mexican stories, thought he might well be meeting Traven, but Croves always held out his hand and announced, 'Croves'. Perhaps Croves's refusal to agree that he was Traven is explained in the simplest way – that he wasn't.

B. Traven: A Mystery Solved

For the last sixteen years of his life, the man who was known as Hal Croves lived in Mexico City. His initial address was 353 Calle Durango, and his second and final home was at number 61 Calle Rio Mississippi, right in the centre of the town. His companion throughout was Rosa Elena Lujan, his agent and translator and the wife he married in 1957. Croves called the room he worked in The Bridge, and thought of the house as a ship. His wife was First Mate and his two stepdaughters Second and Third Officers. Croves died in 1969, and a fragment of home movie is the only living record of the man. He is wearing glasses and seems small and old and meek, a character much at odds with the hectoring, even bullying personality of the writer who typed the name B. Traven at the end of his lengthy letters.

But one thing Traven and Croves had in common. They were secretive. Croves could not bear questions even from his wife, and when they stayed at hotels he encouraged her always to give a false name (returning to the hotel on one occasion, she couldn't remember what name it was she'd invented, and wasn't able to get back into her room). Croves's nationality was a matter for speculation. His passport said he was a Mexican but he became a Mexican as late as 1951, and before then – as the journalist Spota had discovered – his papers gave his birthplace as Chicago. The way he spoke English ought to have offered some clue to his origins, but there again the evidence was conflicting. One of Croves's friends told me she thought the accent was German, another said it was Scandinavian. One morning in Mexico City while I was talking to Señora Lujan (Mrs Croves), she remembered there was a tape-recording in the house. Her daughter had idly turned on the machine one evening as her stepfather had been talking. Mrs Croves fitted the tape on the spool and the voice of Croves who might be Traven filled the room. But there was a distance and indistinctness about the sound, as though the man knew that a day would come even after his death when he must be specially careful to deceive. It was a 'foreign' accent, that was all. His widow believed he was American but then he was typing in German one day and she looked over his shoulder and said, 'But darling, you told me you didn't know any German,' and he simply looked up, stared at her and said, 'I don't ...'

What about the language in which the Traven stories were composed? Bernard Smith was an editor at the American publishing firm

B. Traven: A Mystery Solved

of Alfred Knopf and remembers the day the English manuscript of *The Death Ship* found its way on to his desk:

'It was written, I surmise, as a direct word-for-word literal translation from the German language, because the sentence structure, the paragraph structure and so on was really German. Whereupon I rewrote the first twenty or twenty-five pages of *The Death Ship* and sent them to him. And back came a letter from him saying he was enormously enthusiastic and I had a free hand to do the whole book. I don't want anyone to misunderstand what the nature of the rewrite was. It was not any literary contribution from me – that is to say, I didn't add anything to his narrative or to his characterizations, I merely put his literal translation from the German into acceptable English.'

The Death Ship had originally been published in Germany in 1926, and this and other Traven manuscripts (*The Bridge in the Jungle, The Treasure of the Sierra Madre*) arrived at the Büchergilde Gutenberg – the left-wing publishing house which first brought out the Traven books – written in German. But the German used by Traven is something of an oddity. A student of both Traven and the German language reported that he had taken a passage of forty pages and found over two hundred barbarisms of style – once every second page, on average, there was a glaring error in simple German grammar.

Odd English, odd German. As our final unmasking was to show, there was an uncomplicated, even technical explanation for this ...

The man who called himself Torsvan and later called himself Croves first emerges in Mexico in 1925. The following year he was a member of an archaeological expedition to the jungle region of southern Mexico, the Chiapas. The language and culture of the Indians were Torsvan's passion, and this was the first of many journeys he made to the Mexican jungles. Now it happens that many of the B. Traven stories are set in these same jungles and tell of the Indians in terms that suggest a reworking of their own folk myths. Does this mean that Torsvan who was later to become Croves actually wrote the books of B. Traven? If he did, then a further mystery has to be solved.

If Croves was the author of the work of B. Traven, why did production of the Traven books all but dry up round about 1939? For Croves – who turns up under this name in the early forties – was alive and well and lived for another thirty years. New editions of old Traven material continued to appear during the Croves era, but the texts had been tampered with, German names and references were expunged in what looked like a determined attempt to blur the past. A trickle of new short stories came out in cheap magazines, and there was one long novel called *Aslan Norval*. This book was submitted to several publishers, all of whom turned it down on the grounds that it was unrecognizable as the work of B. Traven. In Germany there were those who took it to be a forgery, and as the Traven scholar Robert Goss has said: if Croves *was* B. Traven, why couldn't he write like B. Traven?

Perhaps the gift had deserted him, perhaps he was written out, perhaps age had diluted the talent. But it must be remembered that Croves invariably denied that he *was* Traven, even going so far as to put it about that Traven as a separate individual didn't exist, that his work was the joint product of two men. This notion sponsored by Croves himself is specially enticing to all who, loving a mystery, love to give it a further twist: what if the work of Traven was actually experienced by one man and written down by another? And if the writing half of that literary duo disappeared in 1939, it would explain why the other partner produced so little.

But if the story of Traven contains two men, it now has to make room for a third. He bears an equally strange name but is a real – even an historical – figure. Ret Marut was a German anarchist, a member of the Revolutionary Workers' Soviet in Munich which had been put down by the authorities in 1919. The day after Croves died in 1969, his widow announced that her husband Hal Croves had also been Marut.

What do we know about Marut? He is first heard of as an actor in Germany in 1907: we find his name as a player of bit-parts on playbills that have survived. But later in Munich he emerges as editor and publisher of an anarchist newsletter, *Der Ziegelbrenner* – literally translated, *The Brick-burner* or *The Brick-maker*. The bricks were for the building of a new society, and the magazine which came out during the First World War was the size, shape and colour of a brick – a fact that later in our researches, and to our great surprise, was to prove the determining factor in our discovery of who B. Traven actually was . . .

One aspect of temperament that Marut certainly shared with Traven and with Croves was secrecy. *Der Ziegelbrenner* carried the words 'No visiting allowed. There is never anyone at home', and all correspondence was via a P.O. box number. And though Marut would address revolutionary meetings in Munich, he would only speak to audiences in the dark, when the lights had been turned out.

So Croves, who had been Torsvan, was also Ret Marut. Why therefore had Croves's widow waited until Croves's death to make this disclosure – and why, when he was alive, had both Croves and his wife flatly asserted the contrary? Explaining the contradiction when we visited her in Mexico City, Señora Lujan (Mrs Croves) simply said that she was following her husband's instructions – on his deathbed he had said she might now tell the truth, he was no longer in any danger from his past.

As collateral for her claim that Marut and Croves were one and the same, Señora Lujan showed us a copy of a novel Marut had written, *An das Fräulein von S ...*, published in Munich in 1916 and a very rare book indeed. She had a parcel which she unwrapped: it was a collection of original *Der Ziegelbrenners*, their red covers slightly faded. All were souvenirs of a previous life, given into her keeping by her husband. Upstairs in the room Croves used as a study – The Bridge – hangs a picture. It is a picture of Croves but it is also a picture of Marut, for when Croves died the German newspapers canvassed the possibility that he had been the old anarchist, and Marut's secretary, who was still alive, had unearthed the picture and sent it to Señora Lujan in Mexico City.

When the Munich Soviet had been dispersed, Marut had been taken prisoner by the authorities and condemned to death. But he had escaped and disappeared. Towards the end of 1922 a postcard arrived at an address in Germany, postmarked Rotterdam: 'In a few hours I shall board a ship to take me across the Atlantic and thereby I cease to exist.' That was the latest information on Ret Marut until our own researches revealed more. Thanks to the US Freedom of Information Act, we discovered in documents unearthed from the CIA, the FBI and the State Department that Ret Marut was in London in 1923 and 1924. At the Home Office, following up the references found in the American files, we brought to light two hitherto unpublished photographs of Ret Marut taken by the British police. And that clinched it – the man who was living in London in 1924, on the run from the German authorities, was Croves, was Torsvan and was Ret Marut. He had been arrested for failing to register as an alien, and spent two months in Brixton Prison before being deported early in 1924 on the steamship *Hegre*, a Norwegian vessel bound for Teneriffe via Brixham. And that gets us back to B. Traven . . .

We know from a document in the American consul's office that Marut worked his passage on the *Hegre* and the job he was given was that of fireman. The hero of *The Death Ship* by B. Traven was also a fireman, and the parallel is hard to avoid. But if Marut *was* Traven, the problem is this: Marut could not have arrived in Mexico until the middle of 1924 – yet the manuscript of *The Cotton Pickers*, an account of adventures among the poorly paid Mexican Indians, arrived at Traven's German publishers early in 1925. How could Marut have absorbed so much of a strange milieu that he was able to write an amazingly convincing book about it, *and* earn a living, all in the few months available?

At least two Traven scholars, Michael Baumann and Robert Goss, believe it was impossible. Baumann said:

'There is sufficient evidence, not only in the novels, but also in the one non-fiction work that has been published so far, that the man who wrote in the first person had lived in Mexico for at least ten, perhaps fifteen or twenty years before Ret Marut could have got to Mexico.'

And Robert Goss adds:

'I don't believe it would have been possible for a newcomer to gain the trust and get the inside knowledge that the B. Traven books show.'

Of course, if the Mexican work of B. Traven were the product of two men – one who had already experienced what the other then wrote down – the difficulty would be resolved. Baumann feels there's something in it:

'A Swiss Traven reader had suggested already in 1964 that an American had been what he called the *Erlebnisträger*, which means the carrier of the experience or experiences. He thought it was this American who wrote the original manuscripts of the early Traven novels and stories in English, and that Ret Marut met this man. If there was another man, he was probably an American "wobbly", a member of the Industrial Workers of the World group of labour unions. The first German version of *The Cotton Pickers*, Traven's second published novel in Germany, was called *Der Wobbly*.'

Well, the possibility of this other man haunts the Traven mystery. The idea seizes the imagination. But facts have to be faced. There is no scrap of evidence that such a second man ever existed. And if it is simply a matter of puzzling out how a writer of the first rank might instantly convert a place and a people he had never before seen into high imaginative fiction, then the words 'imaginative' and 'fiction' are the key: the possibility of the experience is already in the imagination of such an artist, the facts simply supply the opportunity. And fiction is not a process of finding out, it is a process of guessing or divination. Señora Lujan has never doubted that her husband was Traven, and she showed us the diaries he kept while in the jungle, which closely parallel the incidents in Traven's books. Marut was Torsvan was Croves was Traven. But who was the man behind the names?

What is it, to find out who someone is? Traven hoped to vanish into his work, to become, as he put it, 'the word'. And of course the work of writers of his calibre tells us more than ever their names and addresses could. But in a purely scientific sense, to find out who someone is is to find out who his parents were. Marut's identity card gave his place of birth as San Francisco, but to claim San Francisco as your birthplace is to ensure that no one can check it – all the records were destroyed in the fire and earthquake of 1906. When applying for an American passport, Marut gave his father's name as William, and from a letter in State Department files we see that the American consul in London carefully studied a photograph of Marut and, perhaps because Marut had come from Germany, was struck by what he took to be a distinct resemblance to a very famous William – the Kaiser.

Was Wilhelm II the father of Ret Marut? Anyone who compares a picture of Marut/Croves/Torsvan with one of the Kaiser's sons, the Crown Prince, will see there is an undeniable similarity. As editor of *Der Ziegelbrenner*, a subversive tract, Marut was never hounded, which might be thought to be curious, and another curious consideration was where the money to keep the magazine going came from. The third oddity was that Marut, a revolutionary, on occasion wrote almost kindly of the Kaiser. Did he have the protection of a great man – Kaiser Wilhelm II – who was doing it all for his natural son?

Even at the time of *Der Ziegelbrenner* there were rumours that its editor had friends in high places. Many years later Croves spoke ambiguously to a journalist: 'Forget the man. What does it matter if he's the son of a Hohenzollern prince?' His widow agreed that Croves looked very much like the late Kaiser's family, and told me that her husband often talked about Wilhelm II. But Croves was full of tales.

At times he told his wife that he was the son of a poor fisherman in Norway who had died before he was born.

I don't believe that either Wyatt as the producer or I as writer of the film and instigator of the project ever really thought we would find out who B. Traven was. We hoped to make a careful record of what was known with the object of turning it into a coherent narrative. And the witnesses we spoke to made it clear that in their view Traven had not so much blurred his tracks as pulled them up behind him as he went along. Lawrence Hill, one of Traven's American publishers, said:

'The problem of writing the biography of Traven has stumped already four or five writers. They keep running into road blocks and stone walls and blanks in the flow of information.'

And the Traven scholar Michael Baumann simply concluded, 'In my opinion we do not know who B. Traven was.' Traveners felt that their avatar had died with his secret intact, and as Bernard Smith, who had edited *The Death Ship* for Knopf, put it, 'I think we know all we are likely to find out, but I am quite certain that we do not know all that ought to be known.'

How strange that having done no more than stray into the competition, we should have won the prize!

We sorted through all the aliases. As Wyatt and I roamed the world interviewing witnesses, the *équipe* at base camp were seldom off the telephone. Names were the man's obsession. He had been Ret Marut, he had been Fred Maruth, he had been Rex Marut, he had been Richard Maurhut, and of course Croves and Torsvan and Traven Torsvan and B. T. Torsvan, as well as B. Traven. Every alias was traced down and in each case there was no collateral. There was no such address or there were no such parents or no such name or no such record. The man passed out names like dud cheques. The police, the authorities, asked him for names and he gave them names. The more he gave them the safer he felt.

With a sigh, we were about to close the file. We had one last name, one last place, to check. It was a name and a place that Marut had given the police in London in 1923. We assumed that like all the others it would be a false trail. As with all the other names, there would be no real person hiding behind it. We sent off a telegram yet again to a place he had claimed to be the town of his birth. Back with unnerving swiftness came a copy of his birth certificate.

We couldn't believe it. From the little town of Swiebodzin on the Polish-German border came the typewritten evidence: Hermann Albert Otto Maximilian Feige had been a real live human being who had been born in that town on 23 February 1882.

Caution asserted itself. Feige was real, but that didn't mean he was Marut. Marut might have borrowed the identity. We looked again at the birth certificate. Marut had told the police the occupation of his father and his mother: his mother had been a mill-hand, his father a potter – and the certificate confirmed it. Would an impostor have known the occupation of the father and mother of someone else, forty years before? We looked again. The mother's maiden name had been Weinecke. On the list of aliases used by Marut, preserved in the police files of 1923, the same name appears – Weinecke. Would an impostor have known so much?

But when we went to Swiebodzin, we found the parallel was finer. In his deposition to the police in London, the man had said his mother was a 'mill-hand'. But in the birth record-book in the town hall at Swiebodzin, her occupation is listed more generally as 'factory worker'. We made inquiries. There was only one place a factory worker could gain employment at the time of his birth: there were no factories in Swiebodzin, there were only cloth mills. Could an impostor have been so precise?

But the deepest chime, the truly pregnant echo, was one that my own ear was the first to register. We knew the man's father had been a potter. Back in Warsaw, we were drinking coffee and I was chatting idly to our Polish assistant, asking about the word *'Cupfe'* – the town hall records for the 1880s were all in German, for all that time Swiebodzin had been Schweibus and a part of Germany. Yes, she said, *'Cupfe'* would be the German word for potter. I said I thought of a potter as a man who made cups and bowls. Yes, she said, but *'Cupfe'* suggested he made other things – tiles, perhaps.

I let out an unholy roar. 'He made tiles. Tiles are bricks. He made bricks. He was a brick-burner. And since the town was German, he was *Der Ziegelbrenner*!'

That, as far as I am concerned, was the moment I knew I had found my Colonel Fawcett, and the assonance I had heard was given its physical location by an elderly citizen of Swiebodzin who told us where the pottery had stood. It was not an ordinary pottery, he said, it had been part of a brickworks where they had also made tiles and earthenware. I said to the man, 'Would a man who made tiles in such a place be thought of as a brickmaker?' The old chap nodded. 'Would he have been called a *Ziegelbrenner*?' The old chap nodded again. 'Yes,' he said, 'he would.'

For me the search was over. Feige was Marut was Torsvan was Croves was Traven. All of us on the expedition had sailed into the heart of the mystery, but the beat of that heart was something I was first to hear, and I claim the moment as my own.

But more was to come. The town hall at Swiebodzin yielded the names of other members of the Feige family. Feige had brothers and sisters and two of them had moved to Germany – Ernst and Margarethe. They would now be very old – eighty-three and eighty-six. But they would be the only two people in the world able directly to confirm what we had discovered. Even if we managed to trace their last addresses, it was a very long shot that either of them would still be alive. But they were. In a tiny village in Lower Saxony they talked to us about the elder brother they had always called Otto.

MARGARETHE HENZE: He was a very self-willed, intelligent boy.
ERNST FEIGE: He was a strange, peculiar boy. He lived in his own world – no one else had room in his world. He never even played with anyone. He was a loner. He would browse through our books – we had quite a few books – he studied them all.
MARGARETHE HENZE: He was very good at school and so he was going to become a priest. The town of Swiebodzin was going to pay for his studies, but our parents would have to pay for his board and lodging. At that my parents said, 'We can't afford it. There are seven children and we cannot afford that.' And so he had to become a locksmith instead. He was an apprentice for four years, and then he joined the army. And after his time in the army – that was when he disappeared. We never heard from him again.

He was a stubborn boy. That stems partly from the fact that he didn't live with us until he was six – he lived with my grandparents.

꙳ And yes – Otto had been a political activist since his earliest days. Margarethe recalled that he planned to rally the village to the socialist cause, and his room was stacked with placards and leaflets. ꙳

MARGARETHE HENZE: And he also planned to make political speeches in the village, and that made my mother furious. That is when he went away, angry. Well, I mean, you can see why – he had invested a lot of work in this project, and then he doesn't have a chance to get it actually off the ground. So he was mad at them.

After Otto vanished, Ernst recalled his mother had received one letter. It was to tell her that he was in London, and about to be deported.

ERNST FEIGE: He wrote to us once – I think to my mother. That is how we knew that he was in England. And then he wrote again saying that he was no longer in England, that the authorities had kicked him out.

Then Margarethe remembered a later occasion when a policeman called at the house to discover whether it was the home of Hermann Albert Otto Maximilian Feige.

MARGARETHE HENZE: One Sunday afternoon about 1922, they came to the house. And afterwards I found my mother in the loo, crying, and I said, 'Mother, why are you crying? What happened?' She said, 'The police were here, they were looking for Otto; he must have done something wrong. And so we said to them: no, he was not our son.' You see, they were afraid that they might get into trouble over him. And since then we've heard absolutely nothing from him.

They then produced two photographs. One had a face that had been stuck on afterwards – the picture had been taken at his mother's silver wedding anniversary, and since Otto had already disappeared, his face had to be cut from another photograph. And the second was an earlier picture of Otto, taken at the time of his confirmation, when he was about fifteen years old. These photographs were of one man. He was Marut, he was Torsvan, he was Croves, he was Traven. Finally, we showed the two old people our photographs of the brother they had not seen for over seventy years. Their recognition was the final endorsement. We had found B. Traven.

MARGARETHE HENZE: What a funny face he's pulling. Yes, that's him.

What Traven always said turns out to be true. He had no personal claim on anyone's attention. He wasn't after all a president or a millionaire or a prince. He wasn't even born in wedlock, since his parents married a year after his birth. He was the son of a humble brick-burner, and no wonder his German (let alone his English) wasn't very good, since the town of his birth was neither Polish nor German but a mixture of both. All that matters about him at last is his work: he hid behind it, vanished into it, and achieved his wish. He became the word.

Only Child

A lady from a woman's magazine wrote and asked me what it felt like being an only child. Well, nothing. Just a number. But then I started having a little think. Maybe the only child is wrongly named – maybe it's the Only Parent. Most of the only children I knew (and there were a lot about in the suburbs of the thirties) made no claim to special status – but one or two did, and looking back I realize they belonged to parents who didn't look like parents.

When you bent down and pushed open the letterboxes of these Only Parents their houses smelt barren, like the houses of spinsters – something to do with a lack of physical movement, as though the dust never got stirred up into the general atmosphere as it does when a child is in the house, but lay heavily in the carpets generating a separate presence. While ordinary children were robbing orchards, Only Parents took their offspring for Walks. When you saw them, you felt they had just met. I wonder if there aren't people who have children yet who never – in some deep or desperate way – relinquish a virgin status?

Suburban Dream

I suppose the last thing anyone might expect would be to find his own ordinary brick and mortar part of someone else's dream. I thought it was something of a plain number coming up when John

Bratby (who'd politely invited me to let him paint my picture) said
he'd lived in the same suburb as I had lived in, when he was a boy.
But the extra dimension was the novel he'd written about it, *Breakfast
and Elevenses*, and before I left he told me the name of the road he'd
lived in. This rang a bell, and I drove twenty-five miles to make sure
it was where I thought it was. I was right. Bratby and I are of an age.
It was therefore an actuarial impossibility that I wasn't romancing a
girl over a gate in Amberwood Rise while ten paces across the road
in Bramshaw Gardens Bratby was doing the same. But while I was
just doing it, he was dreaming it as well. Odd to find your own avenues
and crescents have a bard, that asphalt and pillarboxes and by-pass
roads you had all but forgotten turn up in someone else's song.

Last Visit to Radio Caroline

Radio Caroline was coming out of taxi-cabs and motorcars
and station waiting-rooms. It was going on and on, making low-key
rhubarb noises, as though all the transistors in the world were propped
up on two pillows and badly in need of Parrish's Chemical Food.

'I've got a feeling right now that someone very special is listening,
yes that's you Linda, your letter was wonderful, all in your own words
what you think of your friends and pop and the whole scene and I
think it's fantastic, I really do, I certainly appreciate those letters you
send and on this sunny-type sunny afternoon I know you're going to
flip when you hear this one coming up on the Brand X label –'

The transistors were in a chronic state of bleeding to death. Nothing
the disc jockeys said seemed to have the right number of red corpuscles.

'Is that a promise? From me to you? O K? Right? O K then. I'll have
a guess and say Ann. Am I right? Marvellous. Well Ann here's a lovely
song that's going to be a very big hit for a very lovely artist –'

The voice sounded as though it were being produced not by a mind
but by a pianola-roll.

'He never had the bladdy teeth out,' said someone real, an oval
shiny-faced man in the Harcourt Shipping Caravan, 'in spite of the so-
called dental appointment. See, these fellows do a straight fortnight on

the ship, then a week off, but he dodged out on the grounds of having a dental appointment. Wily bastard,' said the oval man, who was fixing up for me to go aboard, 'teeth or no teeth.' He pressed hard on the stub of a pencil and spoke the words out loud as he wrote: 'Dear – Captain – once – again – I – have – to – ask – for – your – cooperation –' He broke off, his strictures on disc jockeys tempered by a reasonable man's smiling acceptance that the chubby rascals couldn't be expected to behave like you and me – 'Bladdy good at the turntable, though, and as an ex-detective-inspector from Scotland Yard I think I can say I'm a pretty good judge of horseflesh.'

I'd been giving myself continuous infusions of the voices that came out of the transistor all the way down to Felixstowe, and this, my first contact with ordinary speech, made me feel as if I'd got out of bed too soon against doctor's orders. I went down to the quay and boarded the off-shore boat. It was an old tender, breaking out into rusty cold-sores where the sides had bashed into jetties. We shuddered out into the bay with a cargo of eggs, generators and fan mail.

'I love it, it's fantastic. Sensational. I can't find words to describe it, I really can't. How fantastic can you be? It's really beautiful, it really is –'

The transistor voice had started up again, coming from the bridge where the lad in charge was doing the steering. 'I want my Caroline,' said stickers pasted across the windows of the wheel-house.

'On this sunny-type sunny afternoon, boys and girls, don't forget to give Mum a hand with the dishes now will you, then you're all set for coffee, sit back with coffee, have a cup of coffee, really makes you feel great, take it from me –'

Take it from him! The seagulls shrieked derisively as the Nescafé commercial came up. Surely those bland voices were coming from a ghost ship? Some *Marie Celeste* of the advertising world, manned by tape-recorders? Faintly on the sea-breeze came the smell of frying – it seemed impossible that the source of all those plastic voices could produce anything as organic as chips.

'But we're real to them.' One of the seven disc jockeys aboard the *Caroline* put his fork down. 'A girl in Ipswich said I was one of the family. Her mother rushed out of a chemist's shop and gave me a box of chocolates. How real can you get?'

'We wouldn't be impersonated if we weren't real,' another one said. 'A man on Clacton Pier claimed he was me and got a bed for the night. He went off with a pair of her father's socks.'

The jockeys – who are a bit on the tousled side, what with being manacled to the oars for fourteen days at a stretch – manage to strike a faintly reverential note when they talk about the job. But it's combined with a sort of glumness – reaction, perhaps, to the fact that from now on pirate broadcasting is illegal.

'I was in PR,' said Robbie Dale (his spell at the turntable is called Robbie Dale's Diary), 'and I love talking about happiness. What's wrong with saying nice things? Wilson is a dictator, and the unions are ruining the country.'

His colleague, Sir Johnnie Walker (he gave himself the Sir), produced a poem from an admirer:

> 'Good luck to Caroline is what I say,
> May you forever in the water stay,
> Let the Government rave and shout,
> It won't be long before they are out.'

Much moved, Mr Dale said, 'They're like that. If we so much as say we're out of tea, they send us pounds of the stuff.'

Squashed into the studio amidships, a space the size of a fortune-teller's booth, the jockeys grumbled like human beings. But when the man on duty had to introduce another record, he held up his hand for silence and opened his mouth – the mouth that a second before had shown itself capable of real speech – and fetched out of it a ribbon of sunny upbeat drip-dry cadences that wrapped itself round the possibility of dissent like insulating-tape.

Mr Walker had once sold cars. 'But then I realized there was a whole world outside,' he said, 'where you could get through to people.' What happened after the people had been got through to? Mr Walker looked out from his Ivy Compton Burnett coiffure and said warily, 'What do you mean, what happens?'

I chugged back to Felixstowe and Caroline drivelled on.

'Now I'm dedicating this to a special kind of person, and I think this is the first time this special kind of person has had a record dedicated to them. That special kind of person is a divorced person, and I want to say to all divorced persons that you mustn't feel lonely just because somewhere along the line things didn't work out for you –'

A voice with deep-down shine and an uncomfortable geniality running through it like a fold in a carpet. A voice dedicated to endorsement, beamed to schoolgirls and lonely women in kitchens. The voice of Radio Anaesthesia, tranquillizing the young in the interest of trade, and offering heartsease to the obedient consumer.

Books on the Box

When some years ago I conducted an arts programme on BBC 2 – a series called *The Look of the Week* (a title so exquisitely devoid of meaning it was hard to remember, and thus often rendered as *The Look of the Irish*) – I found it was always the book which was resisted. Cornelius Cardew and his Savoy Orpheans (though time may have blurred the name of the ensemble, the music was unforget-table, featuring as it did a soloist who with unflinching seriousness tore strips of paper in half, very slowly, close to the microphone) – Mr Cardew's mouse-like assault upon the senses was greeted in the studio with cautious reverence. This response bloomed into a sort of moral radiance when the subject was an exhibition of children's paintings, though on this occasion my own black heart lifted once only – when the pundit who had been selected to winnow the blotchy harvest proved he had blood in his veins as, with an audible groan, he turned to one of those present and asked in tones of awful sincerity: 'Doesn't your heart sink at the sight of all that sugar-paper?'

Scarcely less welcome were well-publicized efforts to sell unusable furniture (Fun Areas were in vogue that year) and Jean Tinguely's self-destroying machines (God, how old-fashioned they seemed, the obverse in simple banality of impossible Victorian 'inventions'). These induced a delicious vertigo in susceptible members of our team. But try and pass a book on them and they gave imitations of Marshall McLuhan out for a laugh among the peasants of the electronic village, and getting it by suddenly running into the idiot Caxton.

Sharing as I did the editorial function, it was not presumptuous of me to propose a book now and then, but, unless there was a possibility of the book yielding some sort of open hostility, I found it difficult to hold anyone's attention. I think we did the Arts Council grants to authors on the simple grounds that whoever got them ought not to have got them. Do I recall Mr William Gerhardie, one of the recipients, saying he would spend his on wine-gums? I may have got that slightly wrong, but I think he would have excused the compliment. I was driven to enlisting the aid of the then Head of Department, a man born with a fence stitched to his backside, to ensure that the last and most interesting volume of the letters of Joyce was given an airing. True, there was no argument about Isherwood, but he was a rare bird in those days, and we exhibited him on the box a little as though we thought the box was a barrel. Ah – and I once got them to do a new poem by Auden, read aloud by the poet himself, *but only half of it.*

We were deep in a period when otherwise quite sensible people spoke of certain subjects as 'visual' – by which they meant suited to television – and of certain other subjects as not 'visual' – by which they meant unsuited to television. None of those who thought in this way recognized the essential sentimentality of the distinction: all subjects are visual, unless life is taking place in the dark. Simple communication (sharply to be distinguished from 'art') improves as it approximates to the multifarious aspects of the reality it seeks to give account of. Those who feel it is the natural condition for someone talking about a book not to be seen (as they *are* seen on television) are forgetful of the terms on which they live their daily lives. If there is a realer reality to be had in what is heard but not seen, then the telephone has its place. Nor can we omit the morse code or the tom-tom.

I came closer to the book, on television, with *Take It or Leave It*, another programme masked by an impenetrable title. Here the assumption was that books were O K if used as props for a parlour game. An insulting premise, but one that worked. The formula was simple: people identified authors from brief extracts, but this was only a short fuse to get the conversation going, and the conversation – not chat, actual conversation, with people offering opinion and exchanging ideas, and a minimum of wooden ha'pence – wasn't bad.

Of course, the incidental novelty was there. The pleasure of giving someone like Cyril Connolly the opportunity to confuse *Scouting for Boys* (awarded the Iron Jelloid prize for prose most likely to purify the blood) with late-period Hemingway was undeniable, the chance of someone mistaking part of a story from *Woman's Own* for Jane Austen was slight, but always a possibility, and the cadence of John Betjeman's 'I say, it's awfully good, isn't it?' or alternatively, if something featuring the name Ivan was read out, a cautious 'We-e-ell ... it's

certainly Russian' (since the title of the programme didn't mean
anything anyway, Betjeman said it ought to be called *Money for Jam*)
– these were incidental felicities that nobody sneezed at. Indeed, there
were moments when for the chairman the fun became almost sadistic:
to sit by while Mary McCarthy and the editor of the *TLS* were unable
to identify a piece from *Henderson the Rain King* – when that very week
they had given Saul Bellow the Prix Formentor – and to prolong the
flounder until they were too far from the ship to be thrown a life-belt
– well, Gilles de Rais wasn't in it.

But the great thing about *Take It or Leave It* was the fact of the books
being at the centre of all. Books were being turned to, their substance
was being entered into, and that was rare. In radio and television the
convention has been that books are somewhere you depart from; the
unspoken axiom has been that all books are equally consumable, and
that every book can be treated as though it were a simple variant of
the biography of a lone adventurer who has crossed Herefordshire on
a pogo-stick, something to be mugged-up from the blurb, and never
to be referred to again after your first question has established that
you've got the right bloke.

The ultimate horror generated by this premise rose up before me one
early morning on the *Today* programme. A book was thrust into my
hand, the author was coming in live to the Oxford studio, how did his
new work throw light on, well, premarital sex, the Common Market,
Women's Lib, Sir Keith Joseph and the price of tomatoes? Three
minutes for the interview, three and a half at most. I looked at the title –
Ulysses on the Liffey by Richard Ellmann. I've taken a fence or two in my
time, but I baulked at this one. The editor claimed he had been lum-
bered with the fatuity by someone who hadn't appreciated the scholarly
nature of the work – but how could we stave off the professor without
offending him? Already he would be on his way to the self-manned
Oxford studio, eager for a *causerie* which would prove more people
wanted to hear about James Joyce at eight o'clock in the morning than
he might at first have supposed. I prayed for a miracle, and it seemed
I'd got one – Ellmann didn't turn up. 'Perhaps he cycled past the studio,
mistaking it for a grain store,' said the editor, failing to look me in the
eye, 'or maybe the apparatus defeated him.' I afterwards learned the
editor had made a clean breast of it, telephoned the professor and admitted the book was too good for us. Ellmann's good humour, on this
occasion, was more than we deserved.

Sleep Doth Murder Macbeth

Falling asleep in public is somehow shocking. I don't so much mean the way in which you fall asleep in a railway train and wake up dribbling and then try to assume a preternaturally intelligent expression, as though you'd been brooding as an alternative to the higher calculus – nor even the way you fall asleep at concerts, and try to turn the tell-tale jerk of the chin into a sort of natural, even masterful, twitch symptomatic of the true connoisseur. I'm thinking of those times when to fall asleep looks like an unforgivable comment on everyone else.

I was discussing this with the author Leslie Thomas, and he said he'd been at a dinner party the night before and the man opposite had gone to sleep actually at the table, half way through the meal. What troubled Thomas was the fact that the man had only one arm, and Thomas couldn't get it out of his head that the arm had been eaten by the lady next to him, and the man hadn't noticed because he'd been asleep.

At the Greenwich Theatre once, I was more slept against than sleeping. The lady on my left dropped off the instant the play (*Oedipus at Colonus*) began, and just as instantly dropped her head on my shoulder. Since she was a perfect stranger, politeness enjoined that I should not disturb her, but this was achieved at some cost, since we were sitting in the front row, it was an apron stage, and all the actors were going round thumping the stage with bits of stick, and it seemed to me thumping ever harder as they tried unsuccessfully to get what they obviously supposed was my wife to wake up. Miss Siobhan McKenna in particular, who was playing Jocasta, approached the very lip of the apron, eyes blazing with fury, and roared 'Ho, *Thebes*' in a voice like thunder, but it was no good. The lady woke up refreshed at the interval and simply said to me, with real pleasure, 'That was lovely.' Later, Paul Eddington, who had been in the audience and awake, said he was surprised 'Ho, Thebes' hadn't done the trick, because Ellen Terry had once been slumbering peacefully at a performance of the same play, and when Jocasta shouted 'Ho, Thebes' Ellen Terry woke with a start and cried in piercing tones, 'Edie, quick – there's someone in the house.'

But nobody uses sleep as a weapon to more deadly effect than my friend Philip Purser, television critic of the *Sunday Telegraph*. On being forced by some friends to view their home movies, Purser not only drowsed as soon as the lights went down, but the sofa on which he was sitting being a low one, he rolled quietly off it, and when the lights were switched on again he was discovered in the foetal position on the hearthrug, fast asleep. But Purser's greatest coup – unequalled in every way, but above all in his choice of victim – was to fall asleep when interviewing Noel Coward. Coward pretended he thought he'd fainted, but only because he couldn't bring himself to face the truth! People said Coward's legendary poise received a blow on that occasion from which it never completely recovered.

The Leisure Horse

Leisure's a ghastly thing – lei-shah, you can't even say the word without sounding like Arthur Augustus D'Arcy, who did you ever hear using it in ordinary conversation? – leisure makes me think of a terrible horse we once got landed with in the west of Ireland. 'He isn't the class of baste ye'd find in the Royal Enclosure,' said the proprietor, somewhat obscurely, 'but point him the right way, he'll go for ever.' The horse turned its head moodily and clamped its jaws in the speaker's thorn-proof. 'Pat, Pat, he has me by the shoulder-pads,' cried the proprietor. 'Lay a touch of the window-pole across his shnout.'

The plan was to shuffle about the place in this caravan, do a bit of fishing, play golf, but the horse destroyed time, he ate it, he consumed the hours, swallowed them like a vacuum cleaner. We'd get the rods up at last, just about the time we had to set off for the cooked-meat shop to buy our lunch, after a morning spent leaning against the horse, trying to get him out of the shafts. We had to pull the caravan off him backwards, like a vest, while he stood in the middle of the road, a hairy four-legged slag-heap, blotting out the possibility of enjoyment, radiating dullness.

He followed us down lanes and out into High Streets, as if he were blaming us for something, as though he were exacting a penalty. We urged him to go back to the van, speaking in low, guilt-ridden voices, not wanting anyone to hear. We turned on him and pushed him in the chest, like a family desperate to get the mad brother back into the attic before the guests arrived. But he plodded on, staring at us through the plate glass of sausage shops with a strangely collected air, as though trying to fathom the conundrums written up on the windows in dripping: FALLING IN LOVE WITH OUR COOKED MEATS, or (what seemed like the ultimate paradox) LONG FEET FOURPENCE, SHORT FEET EIGHTPENCE.

We were torn between wanting him to die and wondering whether his death could be laid at our door. He came to dominate not only our time but our emotions: if we'd been nice people, would we have felt ourselves encumbered by him? If we'd been people who knew how to have holidays, would we have found ourselves without the landing net at crucial moments, and blaming it on him? Would we have come back from the pub carrying bottles, approaching the horse – going up to him in the darkness, faces contorted with rage and frustration – to shout, 'What have you done with the bottle-opener?'

In the ad they'd sent us about this horse-and-caravan thing, they'd gone on a lot about what they kept on calling Leisure, and now my long-nourished suspicions about the word – if it meant something nice, why did it have such overtones of obligation, why did it sound as if it was something you had to live up to? – were confirmed. Leisure meant being landed with a horse you didn't want, Leisure meant getting involved in rituals that gave no satisfaction.

Now, I believe that secretly everyone knows this – but being brought up to accept that anyone who acknowledges the fact is at best mad, at worst sinful, they dissemble. You get people lying on beaches in their thousands, enduring the hideous blandness because they think it is expected of them. Fun is something else – Fun is just enjoying yourself, but Leisure is mixed up with virtue. Put your head into the silence of a hotel dining-room, where the ghost of pleasure has receded, and you see it: people chewing in a trance of diligence, sunburnt

captives shouldering the dead weight of Leisure in the vague conviction that marks may be awarded. People smile as they set off for Calais
(anticipation being the better part of pleasure), but those smiles
cannot match the smiles of the people who are coming back – their
exile is ended, their sentence served, and they pass out of the prison
door of Leisure, released into the freedom of their real lives.

You can tell people about the horse, they sympathize. Complain
about hot weather and they get embarrassed. Once we went to
Malaga, and it was too hot. After three days I said, 'We don't have
to stay if we don't want to.' So we came back. When we told people,
they quickly interrupted, butted hurriedly in, pressing explanations
on us like loans – we were ill, the food had been filthy, a revolution
had been imminent, we were worried about our children. No, we said,
it was too hot. Men stared uneasily over the heads of their wives,
women blushed and tittered, edging away towards other groups as
though a trial of their virtue were imminent. But what was causing
the embarrassment was not our infringement of the sacred articles of
the Travel Supplement (in which heat is the Grail, it is never too hot)
but sheer unbelief: people felt we were admitting to some exotic and
irrelevant misdemeanour – say, throwing artichokes in church – with
the object of drawing attention to ourselves. We shut up after that,
and told lies about it.

Leisure was at its apogee the day we took the horse back. People
sat at their devotions in traffic jams, for it was Bank Holiday, and
Leisure swathed the world like a winding-sheet. Browsing through the
day-old paper, I came across a headline that gave the game away –
TRAINING FOR LEISURE. So it was something you had to be trained
for, like fleas! The article had the strained, bright tone of a parson who
is trying to tell you that Death is simply an enjoyable prelude to
something nicer. You got the impression the writer wanted you to feel
that Leisure was something you'd been given because you deserved
it – something you'd earned through hard work and obedience: but
as usual with this sort of evangelistic journalism, the effect was simply
to make you feel that if Leisure was something the Authorities were
offering as a gift, then they'd probably pinched it from you in the first
place.

We stopped outside the stable yard, and the proprietor said, 'Would
you like to keep him another day? No extra charge.' But the poor horse
had been transfigured – he was now the Leisure Horse, a relative of

the Night Mare, symbol of all that had been keeping us from the pleasures of not being on holiday. We thanked the proprietor, but shook our heads.

Lower Pleasures

When the last election was being fought, the coverage was so comprehensive it seemed to destroy everything else, I found I was terribly grateful for small instances of individuality. My friend Bridges wrote and told me that the two little girls next door were having a bath with a visiting small boy. As the various mothers were soaping and lathering the trio, one of the little girls – contemplating what was evidently her first sight of the male anatomy – said in a small appalled voice to the other, 'It's a good job it doesn't grow on his face.' When I read this from Bridges, I recognized with relief that we aren't just voters after all.

P. W. J. Oldroyd of Acton – for no better reason perhaps than that he, too, wanted to remind himself of the peculiarity rather than the predictability of the way we all are – drew my attention to a notice in a local park that announces 'NO CARPET BEATING BEFORE 6 A. M.' I rejoice. Not that I believe getting up early to beat carpets in public stunts your growth, but the prohibition hints at something more magical than any election promise or the opinions of three experts weighed for balance by a visiting apothecary.

He also told me that, in Bournemouth, cast-iron plaques inscribed 'UPPER PLEASURE GARDENS' have had the word 'Pleasure' deleted – a natural consequence, Oldroyd believes, of the earlier decision to erase the word 'Pleasure' from the other plaques which read 'LOWER PLEASURE GARDENS.' You probably remember yourselves how the thunder of feet disturbed your childhood slumbers, as *le tout Bournemouth* raced at nightfall to the gardens where the lower pleasures were to be had, and how the noise didn't compare with the thin tread of the righteous, plodding to the Upper Pleasure Gardens in the early dawn, all carrying their carpets to the ritual beating – prompt at six.

The rather awful thing about the election coverage was the way it actually did a lot of covering: it was drawn up like a winding-sheet over the whole world. The news I got from Bridges and Oldroyd poked up through it like primroses.

Food Talk

There is a certain time of year when an unmistakable trill or tootle is heard, and it is the voice of the *Good Food Guide*, newly hatched as it always seems from the glove pocket of a Rover motorcar. The bird-like warble of the prose is as characteristic as it is endearing – who else would speak of 'immature sauces' or note that occasionally 'a flavour lapses into aggression'? I particularly like the image conjured up by the phrase 'Imagination ran riot in the salad' – perhaps a small door opened in the heart of the lettuce and led you into Wonderland. In Wiltshire, the new edition breathlessly informs me, 'a fussy eater was deeply moved even before he got to the home-made ice-cream' – but since he had already consumed cream of fennel soup, plaice poached in herbs, Magdalen venison with Anna potatoes, carrots in vermouth and buttered swede, deeply moved is what he might look forward to being. Food seems to unhinge some people. 'Our guests,' says one prattler, 'talked all the way home to Munich about their Sole Belle Gabrielle' – and on arrival were soundly banged over the head with a German sausage, one hopes.

Well, I once tried to parody a *Good Food Guide* entry ('The Three Jolly Gallstones, W8 – "Memorable muffins," says one enthusiastic inspector. Mrs Rhomboid still treads her own grapes, but do go properly dressed – George Rhomboid insists on regimental ties and no smoking before the loyal toast.'). But there's no beating the real thing, with a restaurant near Oxford Street run by a family called the Wees, and specializing in marinated bracken shoots, and another not far away where they not only don't have a licence, you mustn't bring your own drink because, says the *Guide*, 'they disapprove'. The book has always been rich in the idiom of the middle classes, from the elderly trio who apparently started a meal in Harrogate by plonking a family-sized bottle of Milk of Magnesia on the table and asking for tinned carrots, to the Hampstead blurbies who once contributed the deathless line 'the duck pie had us gasping with pleasure'.

But are the middle classes still spending their own money on the marinated bracken shoots and the duck pie? I ask because there's a sort of unnatural airiness not just in the *Good Food Guide* but in all food writing. When it comes to listing what went wrong, the lukewarm whitebait and the soggy sprouts are dismissed with an uncaring wave of the hand, a royal casualness, which I associate not with the rich but with people who aren't using their own cash, people who are using plastic, people with expense accounts. I have a feeling that poor service and disappointing food still rouses the rest of us to a pitch of fury, but leaves food writers no more than faintly amused, because in *their* case Farouk pays. I think I'd make it a condition of service of a restaurant critic that the meals he ate were to be paid for out of the fee he negotiated, not reimbursed as expenses. That way, I'm certain the articles would be shorter and the *Good Food Guide* thinner. Nothing makes you more discriminating than paying for it yourself.

Tannous Oblige

True politeness is a commodity in short supply at the best of times, but I came across a sample of gem-like purity. My wife and I were in the elegant shop of Mr Tannous in the Fulham Road, choosing some material to cover a sofa with. On every hand, silks and satins from the ends of the earth, sofas and armchairs that were monuments to the upholsterer's art. We thumbed through the patterns, made a choice, and were about to leave when the heavens, or rather the brown paper bag in which my wife was carrying a pint of milk, opened, the bottle crashed to the floor, shattered into a dozen ugly pieces, and *the* most enormous, most accusing stain spread, as only milk can spread, over the sumptuous carpet of this Aladdin's cave. It was one of those moments when you think if only the last minute could be rolled backwards like a film and we could do it again and make it come out differently. We babbled our regrets, the hot blood mounting in our cheeks, our feelings compounded by the way we knew *we'd* feel if someone had done the same on our carpet. But Mr Tannous's courtesy knew no bounds: with never a glance at his despoiled floor, he looked at his watch, and with some anxiety said, 'Good Lord, it's after half past five. Where on *earth* will you get another bottle?' *Exeunt omnes* ...

Infernal Combustion

I suppose the start was a terrible old motorbike such as they must have used for carrying messages at Agincourt – it called for a special style of riding because the hand-change kept jumping out of gear. This meant you had to drive with one foot up on the tank, holding the lever in place. But to the group of sixteen-year-olds who owned it, the machine was magic because it actually went – it didn't go far and it didn't go for long, but it was the first machine any of them had ever owned which didn't need to be pedalled – and as each of them took a turn riding it round the suburb they roared with pleasure, like Early Man.

It didn't last long because we were pounced on by one of those ill-natured father figures in police uniform who are always being got the better of by fly moggies in American cartoons. A licence was only one of the things we didn't have, and we were hauled up in court, charged with driving without tax, licence, insurance, audible warning of approach, brakes or lights.

We tried a bit of barrack-room lawyery about the audible warning of approach, because what with the stand on which you propped the bike up being loose and dragging along the ground at the back the warning of approach wasn't just audible, it was deafening. One of the lads wanted the sparks it produced taken into account on the no-lights indictment, but the magistrate charged us £1 each and we left the court feeling more or less baptized.

It wasn't until I was in the Army doing National Service that I managed to get myself into the driving seat of something with four wheels. 'Any of you lads drive?' asked the tubby little Captain. 'Sir!' roared the whole platoon, but I happened to be nearest. 'All right – just back her out,' he said.

Well, it was a three-ton lorry and all I had to do was move it backwards ten feet, but I felt it was a start. I got the thing going by a lucky pull at the right knob, managed to push the clutch in and not the brake, but gambled on reverse and lost. The lorry just went slowly forward and ground its bonnet against a brick wall. Believe it or not, the same situation arose a couple of days later, and I was practically in the driving seat before the Captain shouted, 'Get him out – I must be barmy.'

But when I got to Africa as a fully fledged Second Lieutenant and fell into the job of Station Transport Officer, my L-days really began.

I used to work with an elderly Corporal called Balch, who relished rules as only an old soldier can, but at the same time – and though the psychology seemed funny to me at the time (I was only nineteen), it became a lot clearer to me later in life – had a taste for urging other people to break them.

You weren't allowed to drive if you were an officer, but on the way down to the rifle-range with a lorry-load of African soldiers Balch said, 'You going to take her, Rob?' (I used to plead with him, 'Look here, Balch, why don't you call me Sir once in a while?' but he was so senior in every way except rank it was like having an argument with your father.) I said, 'I don't know if I can.' '*What!*' (I can't describe the scorn Balch managed to work into that harmless expletive – he used it a dozen different ways, all beautifully effective.) I said, 'All right, shove over.' He sat in the passenger seat as though life hadn't anything richer to offer him than the sight of me trying to move off with the hand-brake on.

The chaps in the back didn't know what was afoot, but when they were laid flat on their backs by the alacrity of our start they must have guessed. Actually, once we were on the move I didn't do so badly, at least while we were on the tarmac. But soon we had to turn off on to a mud track, and what I hadn't grasped was that you had to slow down if the surface was bumpy.

I kept my foot down and the lorry started to suffer from a sort of earthquake. 'What's the matter with it?' I shouted above the screaming of the Africans in the back. 'The bloody driver,' shouted Balch, as if the one thing he'd tried to do was dissuade me from having a go. 'You twicer,' I shouted, and took my eyes off the road just long enough for the near-side wheels to plunge into a ditch. The lorry gave an almost human groan and lurched about like the hero of a desert film towards the end of the last reel.

It went into the ditch, then it came out again, and then – all this seemed to happen absolutely independently of me, though I still had hold of the wheel and Balch was grabbing for the hand-brake – all of a sudden we were careering across the rifle-range in the teeth of what appeared to be hand grenades. Amid the most frightful bangs and the moans of the soldiers in the back, the lorry stalled and I recall myself shouting – my ears go a dusky red even as I write the words – 'Hold your fire, we are your friends.'

The OC – who was in charge of the group who were making the bangs – opened the near-side door and said, 'Balch, you're after a bar to that MM.' 'Sir, no Sir,' roared Balch, sitting bolt upright. 'Mr Robinson,' said the OC, who fancied himself in the sarcastic line, 'thanks to your timely intervention, the Indians have dispersed. Fortunately,' he continued acidly, 'we were only using thunder-flashes.'

He stalked away and I looked at Balch. 'I wish I had one of those thunder-flashes,' I said, 'because I know just where I'd stuff it.'

Movies in the Morning

The first time I went to a press show I was thrilled to bits at the prospect of meeting film critics, and I nearly burst into tears when I was made to shake hands with the first one and he was carrying a string-bag full of vegetables.

When he sat down he pushed his hat to the back of his head, but didn't actually take it off until after the credits. Culturally speaking, I was feeling pretty insecure: I knew I didn't have to go to the press shows, because the editor I was working for thought reviewing was no substitute for the real business of life, which was interviewing film stars, and I dare say this made me demand more of film critics than they were going to be able to offer. I wanted to feel I'd made it with the intellectuals, but this man's string-bag had two marrows in it, and when the lights came up I could see he was also carrying a cauliflower and a packet of Daz.

I could have murdered him. When he got up I saw he hadn't

bothered to take his overcoat off, and there were deep transverse creases in the herring-bone that suggested years of creative sitting. I got the feeling that films were incidental to his real purpose in life, which was to persuade onlookers that they were honorary members of his own household. When he walked out into the street, I looked sharply at his trouser-bottoms to see if he'd got his pyjamas on underneath.

I must have been feeling fairly paranoid at the time, because I found myself extending this principle, and every morning at the Odeon or the Empire would descry hidden motives as the critics came in through the cold swing-doors. Something about the satisfied way one of my colleagues took his seat made me know (a) he had never doubted that life was meant to be lived on the feet, but (b) no marks were deducted if you could prove you'd done the resting in cinemas. Another man had taken up film criticism because of the unrivalled opportunities it afforded for barking like an Alsatian. Trained to a hair on Capstan Full Strength, he was in a marvellous position to kid people he was only coughing, but he didn't fool me. Barking against time, he could get in twenty or thirty in the course of an average-length feature, and the last as fresh as the first.

Some days you had the Alsatian, and some days you had the man who came along to spot bad lines and get his laugh in first. Some days you had both, of course – woof, woof, ha, ha, and over everything a dense pall of after-shave bursting silently from the pores of someone I could never quite locate, who had carefully marinated himself in Old Spice for the three days previous.

Of course, it was just me feeling persecuted. I knew the editor didn't give a damn if I pirated the reviews from a one-eyed sailorman, as long as they fitted into a panel two inches square and didn't make his wife feel challenged. No wonder I went round suspecting everyone of wanting to beat me to death with rolled-up synopses.

No one likes to be sat next to at press shows – every man keeps an empty seat between himself and the world, and sits suspended in a caul of solitariness. The people who make the films get very worried about the glacial climate that prevails at press shows and sometimes go out into the street, importuning old ladies to come in and do a bit of chuckling. They hope the chuckling will make the critic worried about not chuckling himself, and perhaps nudge him into suspecting his own responses rather than the film's.

Not a bad scheme in theory, but it never seems to work. For one
thing, the undeclared reason a critic puts up with having to give
coherent accounts of films not themselves coherent is that he's never
got over being allowed into a cinema for nothing. If he finds the place
swarming with old ladies who not only haven't paid, but don't even
have to form an opinion, it makes him very sensitive. The old ladies
rustle contentedly, and at the end clap enthusiastically even if the film
has been run backwards. This, and the presence of ice-cream girls,
makes a critic savagely indignant, as though a role he'd taught himself
to experience as more or less in the star class had turned out to be
below-the-title after all.

Press shows are islands surrounded by lunches, the lunches being
given by the film people in the interests of cheering the critics up. I
didn't go all that much because I couldn't muster the metabolism
necessary for talking to a man with that special sort of animation
which stops him wondering why you haven't said anything about the
film you have just seen, which he directed. But in earlier days I could
do it without getting out of breath and, while eating and drinking free,
felt relaxed enough to take in the anthropology.

The lunches looked human enough, but there was always one
element which let you know, as it were through a megaphone, that
the whole occasion had been flown in complete from Selfridges'
grotto. Once it was a man who produced a pigeon from his shirt before
the critics had finished their mussel soup. He'd been hired to put
everyone in a good mood for the film they were going to see, but the
pigeon got away before he could make it do what he wanted it to do,
and it flew up on to a gilt mirror and sat there arranging its feathers.
The man did a few tricks with burning paper and kept on chatting
about how he liked a good gangster picture and did anyone know
what had happened to Veronica Lake. But he couldn't take his eyes
off the pigeon. When people tried to get the bird down by throwing
it bits of bread, he said irritably, 'Leave it alone, it'll come down when
it's ready.' It was a terribly melancholy occasion, and in their hearts
all the critics knew no film was going to be able to match it.

Perhaps half past ten in the morning is a funny time to go to the
pictures. It's the wrong hour to be looking at those bas-reliefs of
females and chariots, left behind on the walls of cinemas as emblems
of a civilization that perished in 1937. Sometimes they even haul in
a man to play the Wurlitzer, and he tinkers away at strange old tunes

as if he were trying to reproduce in laboratory conditions a happy outing of thirty years ago. No good in the morning. Critics leave press shows with a faint metallic taste in their mouths, as though the machinery which processes the fantasies had slightly tainted the product.

Nicknames

I met a man at a party, and he was introduced to me as Chunky Cartwright. Why Chunky Cartwright is called Chunky Cartwright I don't know, and I hope no one tries to tell me because a little mystery is an exercise-yard for the imagination. I myself was known in Africa for a brief period as Mungo, but that was simply because I'd been seen haggling with a bushman over the price he wanted for his spear, and so Mungo explains itself. But my son has two friends, one called Mucker Metcalf and the other called Masher Merrick, and even the two people themselves seem bewildered when asked *why* they're called thus, as though their nicknames were as absolute as their own existence. Even more elemental are two figures out of a family past known only to my elders – Doodle Dick and Dippy Day. Nobody has ever been able to tell me much about either, since from early childhood every time I've asked them they've tried to tell me but the very thought of Doodle Dick and Dippy Day has made them collapse laughing, and they've never got very much further than saying they were pals of your Uncle Bill and Hooky Walker. They were probably sober-sided men in quiet offices off Upper Mersey Street, but the nicknames turned them into demiurges, like clowns in Shakespeare. Other figures looming out of the mists of time are Bluey Barlow, Cherry Johnson and a boy called Krish whose first name was Justin but was always referred to as Whiffy – Whiffy Krish. Nobody ever makes up nicknames, a nickname is your real identity, jumping out from behind you like an afreet.

Show Business

I had sometimes thought that if there were a single human being able to resist an invitation to appear on a chat show it might turn out to be the Archbishop of Canterbury. But there he was on *Parkinson*. I suppose Cantuar thought he might as well contribute a Christian presence to the thing, but he reckoned without the power this sort of show has to fictionalize everyone who goes on it. Instead of the Christian presence dominating the worship of idols, the Christian presence was converted into one of its active ingredients: instead of the mantle of Augustine covering the show, the show covered it, in the mantle of Narcissus. Here is another funny old gentleman (the picture, the idiom, the style, the arrangements seemed to be saying) willing to entertain us.

I think the Archbishop might have tumbled to all this as soon as he heard he was to be teamed with Norman St John-Stevas. Norman is a work of fiction long before he ever arrives at a television studio, and when the Archbishop heard who was to be his partner he should have realized that what they were really after was a couple of adagio-dancers. Once the Archbishop is available for this sort of gig, it means that show business extends in a seamless integument, right from *Parkinson* to Canterbury, round the Cathedral, and back again.

Public Bath

You turn a corner and see your own bath standing outside somebody else's front door. It happened to me – there it was in Christchurch Street, Chelsea, the absolutely unmistakable object, the bath so big it never looked quite right without a diving-board at one end, the very bath to which over the last fifteen years each of my three children in turn has been reluctant to go, but once in has resolutely refused to get out of – there it was, with the two big taps that look as though they're holding back the Aswan Dam, standing on its end outside some bright spark's dinky new villa. It's a dream-like experience, seeing your own bath in an unfamiliar context – it's like running across your mother in a nightclub. 'What's my bath doing in Christchurch Street?' I asked the builders when I got back home. 'Ah,' said the painter, 'Mr Thing was looking for one of those big old-fashioned ones, so we gave him yours. It's what they call the nostalgia kick,' said the painter kindly. Now it's true I was having this particular bathroom de-natured – an action equivalent to laying your hands on all the five-pound notes you can find, stuffing them into a Gladstone bag, and taking them to the zoo to feed the giraffes – but what I hadn't bargained on was them levering out the actual bath and *giving* it to someone, especially not someone who was going to use it as a period piece. Think how you'd feel if your bath were being *patronized* – how would you like it if you saw it standing outside someone else's house, surrounded by inverted commas? When your bath turns out to be *amusing*, what does that make you? On the other hand, of course, in not being too snooty to accept my cast-offs, Mr Thing is himself rather one down, wouldn't you say? And being a thoughtful sort of cove – I visualize him as the archetypal purchaser of reproduction pub mirrors – he will realize that since his bath used to belong to my children, every time I pass his house I shall be wondering whether he is at that very moment playing with his celluloid ducks.

The Principality of Wittgenstein

I am a tourist in the Principality of Wittgenstein, and since I have long entertained the notion that we only read books we already know, with the object of finding out that we *do* already know (if we didn't already know, how would we understand?), I am delighted that Ludwig himself – I call him Ludwig in jesting earnest of my unfitness to keep his company – points out that the *Tractatus* would only be intelligible to those who knew it before they read it.

My profound mistrust of my own capacity to understand what attracts me led me to take a pocket tape-recorder with me on long train journeys when I was reading the book, to croon into it such of the spoil as I could recover. I had to be able to do whole chunks coherently, otherwise I didn't pass Go. When I first heard the music of that opening bar – 'The world is everything that is the case' – I had the sensation you get in your stomach as a child, coming down from the apogee on a high swing. 'Whereof we may speak, thereof we may speak clearly: whereof we may not speak, thereof we must be silent' – I know it's old hat to professionals, but to day-trippers like myself landmarks like this can take the breath away, like the view from a high mountain.

Russell said that for one acknowledging the limitless reaches of silence, Wittgenstein had a lot to say. But the thrill is knowing that the book begins where the words end. Led through the necessary forest by a magician who believes his secrets to be your secrets too, you emerge startlingly at the farther edge, falling out of the words into a silence that can only be shown. Ludwig had a homely way of making the point: turning up at meetings of the Vienna Circle to explain the *Tractatus*, he wouldn't say anything all evening, just *whistle* excerpts from his extensive classical repertoire. Must have given them a special sort of headache. I had this out of William Warren Bartley's *Wittgenstein*, but I don't like new books about Wittgenstein. I'm jealous of Wittgenstein going public. I was talking to someone who couldn't stand the way everyone else now knew about Malcolm Lowry. Some people you want to keep for yourself.

Lost Books

I doubt if I ever enter a second-hand bookshop in a market town, or prod through the mulch of print on the barrows in Farringdon Road, without the small pilot-light of hope still burning: that this will be the day I open the unappetizing-looking covers of the umpteenth edition of Thomson's *Seasons* or Young's *Night Thoughts*, and find that the binding is simply a folder for a much earlier manuscript, something an unthinking antiquary had tucked away for later consideration and forgotten, leaving me to be the first to decipher the crabbed signature over the unknown play – 'William Shakespeare'. I believe this is a fantasy many people share, and it will happen sooner or later.

The title of the lost play, as a matter of fact, might easily have turned out to be *Duke Humphrey* if the great eighteenth-century collector Warburton, had been a bit more careful. In his library, he had the autograph manuscripts of no fewer than fifty-five plays of the Jacobean and Elizabethan theatre, many of them otherwise unknown, by writers such as Dekker and Marlowe and Ford and Massinger. One of the plays was called *Duke Humphrey*, and it had Shakespeare's name on it. And one day Warburton discovered they had all gone. His cook came to him and asked if he had any more old papers she could take down to the kitchen, as she had got to the end of the last lot. She had used all fifty-five plays to line the bottoms of pie-dishes.

It scarcely bears thinking about – but the whole subject of manuscripts lost, stolen, hidden or destroyed betrays a carelessness that makes your hair stand on end. You would think, having tortured *The Seven Pillars of Wisdom* out of himself, T. E. Lawrence would not have left the manuscript in the station buffet at Reading, 'I've lost the damn thing,' he is reported as very pardonably exclaiming. There were those who said it was a stunt, a further example of Lawrence's unquenchable thirst for publicity. But no one can doubt the genuineness of Carlyle's feelings when he heard that the manuscript of the first volume of his *French Revolution* had been destroyed. I wouldn't have been in John Stuart Mill's shoes, walking up Cheyne Row that evening to tell Carlyle (who had lent it to him) that he had accidently chucked it on the fire. No wonder he took his girlfriend, Mrs Taylor, with him for support. They stayed two hours, and what a dreadful two hours that must have been.

But to see manuscripts being destroyed, and deliberately destroyed, must be peculiarly horrifying. Frank Barber, the black man, watching Dr Johnson tearing the pages out of his manuscript autobiography and piling them in the grate, then hooking part of one of the volumes out of the flames when his master left the room, so that we still have the fragment, rather pathetically entitled *Dr Johnson: His Life from*

Birth to the Age of II. Frieda Lawrence shouting to David Herbert when the postman brought back rejected manuscripts, 'They're all bosh. Nobody wants them,' and flinging the lot on the fire. Thomas Hardy's gardener looking on while Mrs Hardy fed a bonfire with diaries, letters, notebooks, under orders from the dead novelist to make away with the lot.

It is not uncommon, or, indeed, unreasonable, for authors to want to protect their private selves, but to treat your work as a sort of false beard you will be allowed to go on wearing beyond the grave seems a bit hopeful. T. S. Eliot wanted no biographies, but has had them visited upon him. Auden bade his friends tear up his letters, but it seems unlikely anyone has done it. Hardy had better luck, but then he went to the lengths of writing a public relations handout about himself, the manuscript of which he destroyed as fast as his wife typed it out for him, presenting it to his publisher under her name. What an impossible ambition, to hope to revoke your real life by simply rewriting it.

Sir Richard Burton, the explorer, showed no sign of wanting to improve his image, but his wife did it for him. The breath was scarcely out of the randy polymath's body than she burnt many of his papers. A publisher offered her 6,000 guineas for the MS of *The Scented Garden*, but she refused, and it joined forty years' worth of diaries and note-books on the bonfire. John Forster pulped hundreds of letters from Dickens, for fear the yeast of the man's real presence might rise so high it toppled the monument.

The discovery of Scrope Davies's papers in somewhere as mundane as Barclays Bank holds out hope for us all: laundry bills, Byron manuscripts, Shelley poems and sketches of Napoleon by a midshipman who was actually on the *Bellerophon* en route to St Helena – practically a photograph. Some of the material is already on display at the British Museum.

Who will be the first to stumble across that first draft of *The Seven Pillars*, possibly still behind the tea-urn at Reading? And there is a play, called *The History of King Stephen*, entered in the book of the Stationers' Company as by William Shakespeare. Turn out your attics.

Prairie Tortoise

Before dinner three of us were talking about Kissinger, and the rambling discussion went on, I suppose, for about twenty minutes, and it can't have been of a specially high order because I don't remember a word of it except when we got up to go in and eat the woman said, 'Whatever else you say about the man, you can't knock his moustache.' Feeling real interest for the first time, I said, 'Oh, has he grown one?' 'Well, how else would you recognize him,' said the woman. 'Well,' I said, 'um, let's see, well, his funny hair.' 'Oh,' said the woman, 'are there any pictures of him without his cap on – I've never seen any.' It then became clear that while two of us had been talking about Kissinger, she'd been talking about Kitchener, and for twenty minutes none of us had noticed.

I think we only hear what we want to hear. A correspondent told me that as a child she was for a long time confused about the part played in the Anglican communion by a fabulous beast called the Prairie Tortoise. At some point in the service, at Sunday school or school assembly, the congregation would cry out excitedly, 'Let us *hear* the Prairie Tortoise,' and my correspondent says she always hoped that the creature's characteristic whinny might somehow be reproduced. A long time afterwards, running the phrase through her head, she realized there was no such animal, just a pious hope to hear the prayer he taught us. My friend Skinner adds that he often wondered why the service took such a personal turn when the whole congregation would kneel down and groan, 'Pray for us Skinners' – though, he said, he knew the family stood in more than ordinary need of it.

Children make these mistakes all the time, but I was at a party and I was talking to a dentist, and he said he had just noticed Harold Wilson walking through Westminster wearing shoes which, said the dentist, 'I wouldn't gargle in'. This struck me as only slightly odd, because he was after all a dentist and perhaps this was a bit of dental vernacular, perhaps gargling is despised in the profession: you do feel rather mere when you're doing it, much of it going down your chin.

Then I remembered this chap was an Australian dentist, and maybe in Australia they do actually supply you with special old shoes you put on when you do it in case you spoil your good ones. So I said perhaps Wilson was on his way back from doing a bit of gargling and had forgotten to change, and the dentist said, 'What on earth do you mean, gargling, I said gardening.'

Books as Tombstone

Collecting books is perverse. Books are to be read, and if you collect a book you daren't read it, daren't even open it, daren't even put it on the shelf in case the sun bleaches the spine or foxes the endpapers or otherwise makes the book look as though intercourse had taken place. When you collect a book, you put it in a nunnery at birth, and it is never deflowered.

Even as I say all this, I think of my own books and feel guilty because many of them have been waiting to be read for thirty years and the great moment has yet to arrive. I sometimes glance at my shelves and the books seem to turn into an old snapshot that doesn't look like me any more. A friend of mine got the idea his books were his tombstone – that he'd died half way through his own life – so he sold the lot. Just sometimes, the ones I've got look as though they've been hanging around so long they starved to death years ago.

Watch Your Step

I don't think sociologists have given enough thought to the way people walk. Top end of the social scale, people walk as though they aren't walking anywhere in particular, bottom end of the scale, people walk as though they only had one destination. Bottom end, people walk as though the movement were being rented rather than owned outright, top-end walks are always freehold. Bottom-end walks are really forms of marching, top-end people walk as though walking wasn't anything they'd ever had any reason to perfect. I once saw the late Duke of Marlborough walking up the stairs at Christie's and he did it as though if the legs he was using turned out not to suit him he could get dozens more where they came from. You can no more disguise your walk than you can your handwriting: I knew a ballet critic who'd once been a policeman, and he always walked up the aisle at Covent Garden as though he were going to take Giselle's name and address. Middle-aged Frenchmen appear to have funny walks, but that is simply the effect of the curious wide trousers they wear.

A Presidential Address to the Johnson Society of Lichfield

The voice is unmistakable, even to those whose acquaintance with it comes no closer than a book of quotations. 'What, is it you, you dogs! I'll have a frisk with you.' 'Sir, your wife, under the pretence of keeping a bawdy house, is a receiver of stolen goods.' 'Is not a Patron, my Lord, one who looks with unconcern on a man struggling for life in the water, and, when he has reached ground, encumbers him with help?' 'When a butcher says his heart bleeds for his country, he has in fact no uneasy feeling.' Unmistakable, not simply because it is the voice of Johnson, but unmistakable because in its uniquely human reverberation, it is the voice of one individual reaching out to another, *confident* that that other – in all his own individuality, in all his separateness – will be there.

But that was a long time ago. Ever since communication became an industry – ever since communication became communications, and conversation dwindled into something people listed as an interest, along with stamp-collecting or keeping ferrets – above all, since the spoken word was taken into public ownership by the media and began to fill the universe with a sort of roaring – ever since that time, confidence that there is an individual to talk to has waned in exact proportion to confidence that it is an individual who is talking.

Some general voice seems to have dispossessed an immense variety of voices. Though Johnson spoke forcefully, though he spoke – as he said – for victory, he nonetheless spoke as though his voice were one among many, as though he recognized that someone else would always be there to speak after him. To Johnson, speech was as various as the individuals who used it, speech was understood to be one of the principal ways in which a human being identified himself, and what was said – even when it wasn't very interesting – had a special force because it belonged to someone, it was always someone's private property. Now that speech is produced in bulk, in studios, in front of microphones and cameras, that's something that appears to have changed – now that speech has been turned into an amenity and been laid on, like electric light or underfloor heating, it just doesn't seem to belong to anyone in particular, and its idiom is as anonymous as those dull brown envelopes that arrive by second post and seem destined for no one and coming from nowhere.

And if the collective voice belongs to no one, who is it actually talking to? That is the heart of the matter, for if *it's* not there, neither are we – at least, not in the way that Boswell and Dilly and Wilkes and Mr Slater the druggist were there. For Johnson always addressed himself to the particular ear and, in doing that, acknowledged the individual – acknowledged the prime condition of existence, the presence of others. But when speech is turned into a seamless electronic caul which has no beginning and no end, *it wraps us up*, and far from promoting the contact for which Johnson saw it as the prime instrument, it insulates against it. It is not so much a simple gap that separates the uses of speech in Johnson's day from the uses of speech in our own. It is not a difference in degree, it is a difference in kind, a distinct change of purpose. Whatever Johnson wanted speech to do for him, I think we want it to do something else for us.

When I spoke of Dilly and Wilkes and Mr Slater the druggist, I was of course thinking of that dinner party to which Johnson was so cunningly enticed by Boswell, and I suspect that those who cherish that occasion actually have the feeling that they were there too. The presence of the men who made up the party on that night is so powerfully evoked that it reinforces a sense of our own identities. But when, by virtue of the little screen, I appear to be in the presence of disc jockey, chat-show host, quizmaster, anchorman, or politician, I see a mouth that opens and closes but I have no distinct impression that anyone is there. The feeling creeps over me that the smile the man is smiling is a smile he assumes I am smiling too. Should his expression be one of candour, indignation, concern, I seem to sense that it is on his face because he understands it to be on mine. In the house of Dilly the bookseller, each man's responses were his own business, but there is something about the man on the little screen which suggests he has surrendered all *that* to me – that he exists only as a mirror for what he presumes I require. Indeed, he communicates a sense of his own absence as powerfully as the men in Dilly's parlour that May evening in 1776 communicate just the opposite, and sometimes as I sit and watch him, the sense that there is no tenant is so strong I have the bewildered conviction that a bank of unmanned tape-recorders is pretending to take a warm personal interest in me.

Mr Dilly is at home, the man on the little screen is out: he offers himself as an outline in which we are to draw our own faces. But at Dilly's from the very outset there is no question of anyone being consulted about the nature of the entertainment.

BOSWELL.'Mr Dilly, Sir, sends his respectful compliments to you, and would be happy if you would do him the honour to dine with him on Wednesday next along with me, as I must soon go to Scotland.' JOHNSON. 'Sir, I am obliged to Mr Dilly, I will wait upon him.' BOSWELL. 'Provided, Sir, I suppose, that the company which he is to have, is agreeable to you.' JOHNSON. 'What do you mean, Sir? What do you take me for? Do you think I am so ignorant of the world, as to imagine that I am to prescribe to a gentleman what company he is to have at his table?' BOSWELL. 'I beg your pardon, Sir, for wishing to prevent you from meeting people whom you might not like. Perhaps he may have some of what he calls his patriotick friends with him.' JOHNSON. 'Well, Sir, and what then? What care *I* for his *patriotick friends*? Poh!' BOSWELL. 'I should not be surprised to find Jack Wilkes there.' JOHNSON. 'And if Jack Wilkes *should* be there, what is that to *me*, Sir? My dear friend, let us have no more of this. I am sorry to be angry with you; but really it is treating me strangely to talk to me as if I could not meet any company whatever, occasionally.' BOSWELL. 'Pray forgive me, Sir: I meant well. But you shall meet whoever comes, for me ...'

The stratagem Boswell is employing is an elegant one:

Notwithstanding the high veneration which I entertained for Dr

Johnson [says Boswell] I was sensible that he was sometimes a little actuated by the spirit of contradiction, and by means of that I hoped I should gain my point. I was persuaded that if I had come upon him with a direct proposal, 'Sir, will you dine in company with Jack Wilkes?' he would have flown into a passion, and would probably have answered, 'Dine with Jack Wilkes, Sir! I'd as soon dine with Jack Ketch.'

But my point is this – how indelibly Boswell insists on the individuality of all concerned: it is as though, when we hear them speak, they stand before us:

I found him buffeting his books, covered with dust, and making no preparation for going abroad. 'How is this, Sir? Don't you recollect that you are to dine at Mr Dilly's?' JOHNSON. 'Sir, I did not think of going to Dilly's: it went out of my head. I have ordered dinner at home with Mrs Williams.' BOSWELL. 'But, my dear Sir, you know you were engaged to Mr Dilly, and I told him so. He will expect you, and will be much disappointed if you don't come.' JOHNSON. 'You must talk to Mrs Williams about this ...'

Even those at the periphery of these events are distinctly revealed:

'Yes, Sir,' said Mrs Williams, pretty peevishly, 'Dr Johnson is to dine at home.' 'Madam' (said I) 'his respect for you is such, that I know he will not leave you unless you absolutely desire it ... be pleased to consider my situation; I carried the message, and I assured Mr Dilly that Dr Johnson was to come, and no doubt he has made a dinner, and invited a company, and boasted of the honour he expected to have ...' She gradually softened to my solicitations and was graciously pleased to empower me to tell Dr Johnson 'That all things considered, she thought he should certainly go.' I flew back to him, still in dust, and careless of what should be the event, 'indifferent in his choice to go or stay'; but as soon as I had announced to him Mrs Williams's consent, he roared, 'Frank, a clean shirt' ... When I had him fairly seated in a hackney-coach with me, I exulted as much as a fortune-hunter who has got an heiress into a post-chaise with him to set out for Gretna Green ...

There is a directness of address, as though the words were the man, whether it be Johnson who speaks or Boswell or any one of their contemporaries sitting down to entertain themselves and each other with the spoken word. Everything that is said is of a particularity, for speech was an instrument everyone felt it necessary to learn to play. With the advent of electronic communications we hired someone to do it for us, handed over our responsibilities to concessionaires, on the understanding that they would use the facility to offer us endless consoling reflections of ourselves. That is why the figure on the little screen has the effect of a line drawn round a vacancy – it's not his business to be present, he dare not be, since his function requires him only to send back echoes to the audience. How absurd, therefore, to suggest – as we sometimes hear it suggested – that if Johnson were alive today he would somehow be a great success on television! This sentimental notion (as insulting as it is half-baked) is repudiated, even, I would claim, refuted by my thesis, for if the principal source of talk is a large anonymous electronic mouth, what possible use would a man like Johnson be? Present in every particle of himself in all he uttered, he accommodates nobody except himself.

I mentioned a cause where a Probationer (as one licensed to preach, but not yet ordained, is called) was opposed in his application to be inducted, because it was alleged he had been guilty of fornication five years before. JOHNSON. 'Why, Sir, if he has repented, it is not a sufficient objection. A man who is good enough to go to heaven, is good enough to be a clergyman' ... Hence a question arose, whether fornication was a sin of a heinous nature: JOHNSON. 'No, Sir, it is not a heinous sin. A heinous sin is that for which a man is punished with death or banishment.' BOSWELL. 'But, Sir, after I had argued that it was not a heinous sin, an old clergyman rose up, and repeating the text of scripture denouncing judgement against whoremongers, asked whether, considering this, there could be any doubt of fornication being a heinous sin.' JOHNSON. 'Why, Sir, observe the word *whoremonger*. Every sin, if persisted in, will become heinous. Whoremonger is a dealer in whores, as ironmonger is a dealer in iron. But as you don't call a man an ironmonger for buying and selling a penknife, so you don't call a man a whoremonger for getting one wench with child ...'

Such uncompromising identity would not flatter an audience, and audiences are what speech in our time has been adapted to. In Johnson's circle each spoke and listened by turns, and Johnson being first among equals was deferred to. But there was no audience as we know audiences, there was no segregation so that those who are on one side of the microphone do all the talking and those who are on the other do all the listening. When a microphone is handed to a member of an audience, it is a frontier to which that member has been conducted, but it is a frontier he must not cross: *his* duty is to ask a question, and whether that question touches on the moral desirability of the closed shop or the freedom not to wear a seat-belt, the question always sounds like one he would be better off putting to himself. But he turns to the group on the magic side of the microphone, and puts it to *them*, and as he sits down a quartet of mercenaries (three men and one woman, all well known for being well known) will spiritedly act out the arguments for him. The medium supplies a place where audience and performer are joined. That process is an act of surrender on both sides, for the performer gives himself away to the audience – is nothing without it – and the audience in accepting the performer as a validation of its own reality, to some extent switches itself off as it switches *him* on.

No such deputies were required at Mr Dilly's house.

Mr Arthur Lee mentioned some Scotch who had taken possession of a barren part of America, and wondered why they should choose it. JOHNSON. 'Why, Sir, all barrenness is comparative. The *Scotch* would not know it to be barren.' BOSWELL. 'Come, come, he is flattering the English. You have now been in Scotland, Sir, and say if you did not see meat and drink enough there.' JOHNSON. 'Why, yes, Sir; meat and drink enough to give the inhabitants sufficient strength to run away from home . . .' JOHNSON (to Mr Wilkes). 'You must know, Sir, I lately took my friend Boswell and shewed him genuine civilised life in an English provincial town. I turned him loose at Lichfield, my native city, that he might see for once real civility: for you know he lives among savages in Scotland, and rakes in London.' WILKES. 'Except when he is with grave, sober, decent people like you and me.' JOHNSON (smiling). 'And we ashamed of him . . .'

There is that in Johnson's speech which proclaims him in all his parts, so that when we come upon him unawares in the memoirs of those whose company he kept, the sense of this always being the same man is so intense that the moment of recognition can catch the throat with emotion:

I shall never forget [writes Miss Reynolds in her *Recollections of Dr Johnson*] the impression I felt in Dr Johnson's favour, the first time I was in his company, on his saying that as he returned to his lodgings, at one or two o'clock in the morning, he often saw poor children asleep on thresholds and stalls, and that he used to put pennies into their hands to buy them a breakfast.

We know him, on the instant.

Dr Johnson [says Miss Reynolds] was very ambitious of excelling in common acquirements, as well as the uncommon, and particularly in feats of activity. One day, as he was walking in Gunisbury Park (or Paddock) with some gentlemen and ladies, who were admiring the extraordinary size of some of the trees, one of the gentlemen remarked that, when he was a boy, he made nothing of climbing (*swarming*, I think, was the phrase) the largest there. 'Why, I can swarm it now,' replied Dr Johnson, which excited a hearty laugh (he was then between fifty and sixty); on which he ran to the tree, clung round the trunk, and ascended to the branches . . . and down he came, *seeming to make nothing of it.*

Of course, Chesterfield's intention was to diminish Johnson when he said of him, 'He is exactly the same to his superiors, his equals, and his inferiors' – but *sub specie aeternitatis*, what a benison the sentence bestows. In any circumstance, he is the unchanging factor. Sententious or jocular, rebuking or gallant, he is never other than as he last appeared to be:

I went into his room the morning of my birthday once [writes Mrs Thrale] and said to him, 'Nobody sends me any verses now, because I am five and thirty years old' . . . My being just recovered from illness and confinement will account for the manner in which he burst out suddenly, for so he did without the least previous hesitation whatsoever, and without having entertained the smallest intention towards it half a minute before, thus:

> Oft in danger, yet alive,
> We are come to thirty five;
> Long may better years arrive,
> Better years than thirty five.
> Could philosophers contrive
> Life to stop at thirty five,
> Time his hours would never drive
> O'er the bounds of thirty five.
> High to soar and deep to dive,
> Nature gives at thirty five.
> Ladies, stock and tend your hive,
> Trifle not at thirty five:
> For how'er we boast and strive,
> Life declines from thirty five:
> He that ever hopes to thrive
> Must begin by thirty five;
> And all who wisely wish to wive,
> Must look on Thrale at thirty five . . .

'And now (said he, as I was writing the verses down) you may see what it is to come for poetry to a Dictionary-maker; you may observe that the rhymes run in alphabetical order exactly . . .'

When Johnson speaks, you have the impression of entering a life. Each time he speaks, it is another door that opens. But with the little screen, all you can do is walk behind it and nobody is there, you are simply back-stage. The memoirs I have quoted from are recognizably a medium – they carry the message just as distinctly as the electronic voice of our day. But there is an interesting distinction: the medium of the memoir is composed of individual voices, and those individual voices define it, it does not define *them*. No doubt there are those who stand against the homogenizing processes of latterday communications – who try to use the camera and the microphone rather than letting the camera and the microphone use *them*. But they are few enough to be a scarcely visible minority, and in the end they too are used, for their eccentricity may be seen to be licensed, and in permitting them to strain against it, the electronic tide exhibits the irresistible force of its own anonymous flow.

It is a force that flattens the landscape of communication, bulldozing idiosyncrasy, demolishing awkwardness, pulverizing spontaneity. Sometimes as I stand in a pub disobediently not playing on a fruit-machine but actually talking to someone, I begin to feel like some mad smallholder still desperately tilling a small plot while all around him the developers are throwing up sitcom palaces and chat-show tower-blocks and quizgame thru'ways, pausing occasionally to lean on his spade and wonder if there is still anyone out there. I suspect each of us from time to time feels marooned in the electronic nowhere, and at such moments we may find ourselves thinking with a mixture of wistfulness and hope of a day when men actually turned to each other as Johnson first turned to Boswell, and in an exchange of words that celebrated and embraced the possibility of their joint existences, cried, 'Give me your hand. I have taken a liking to you.'

2